the art of
Papercutting

Rotate

the art of
Papercutting

35 stylish projects for gifts, cards & decorations

deborah schneebeli-morrell

CICO BOOKS
LONDON NEW YORK

For Helen Scott Lidgett, my friend and supporter

Published in 2011 by CICO Books
An imprint of Ryland Peters & Small Ltd
20–21 Jockey's Fields   519 Broadway, 5th Floor
London WC1R 4BW   New York, NY 10012

www.cicobooks.com

10 9 8 7 6 5 4 3 2 1

A CIP catalog record for this book is available from the
Library of Congress and the British Library.

ISBN 978 1 907563 79 9

contents

introduction

Papercutting, once a peasant craft, has today become a fashionable hobby. Inspired by the folk-art tradition, crafters have pushed out the boundaries of the technique to produce exciting new designs. But you don't need to buy examples of papercuts when you can make them! The projects in this book will inspire you to discover and enjoy the art of papercutting for yourself.

As a medium, it appeals not only to the skilled, creative, and talented crafter but also to someone who has more enthusiasm than experience. Tools and equipment are kept to the minimum—you can get started with nothing but some scraps of colored paper and a pair of scissors.

Techniques vary, but the most traditional method of creating a papercut is to fold a piece of paper and, with small, sharp scissors, cut out a freehand design, without using a pattern or having first drawn it. The paper is then opened up to reveal a perfect symmetrical design. The best example of this approach is the ubiquitous snowflake that children learn to make.

Papercutting was once a universal peasant art, examples of which appear throughout history and in many different cultures around the globe, from China to the Americas and from southern Europe to Scandinavia. Polish papercuts are very graphic and in bold colors—simple folded designs were used as brightly colored decorations for the home. The beautiful black papercuts from Switzerland are more intricate, often depicting life on an alpine farm. Early American settlers brought the craft with them from the Old World—for example, there are many Shaker papercuts embellished with painting, drawing, and writing. Mexico is another source of brightly colored papercuts, in the form of intricately cut tissue-paper banners that are used to adorn homes at significant festivals, such as the Day of the Dead, which is celebrated at the beginning of November.

Papercutting developed as a peasant craft for the same reason that patchwork did—because it could be made inexpensively from old scraps. Recycled newspapers, letters, wrapping paper, packaging, and many other types of paper that were saved and collected all had their own appeal, and their patterns, textures, and colors became important elements in the designs.

As sources of inspiration for your own designs, original examples of the craft are worth seeking out. Folk art, with its simplicity and lack of sophistication, has an immediate appeal. Also look at modern examples, to see how the craft is evolving. Copying the original designs you find will help you understand how they were made. You will soon add your own style, once you start to feel comfortable with the technique.

I have used a variety of different kinds of paper for the projects in this book. Some have been collected over time because I liked the color, texture, or pattern, but most have been bought from specialist paper shops. Paper and cardstock are sold in sheets, and the precise weight is usually specified. However, to keep things simple I have just indicated whether it should be light, medium, or heavy. You can tell this by handling the sheets before you buy them. Origami paper, which is used in a number of the projects, is extremely lightweight.

If you like paper, you will no doubt be carried away when you visit an art paper store, and will come home with far more papers than you intended to buy. You can then allow these papers to inspire your own papercut designs! But even when you are still just embarking on your first project from the book, I hope you'll discover the same pleasure that I have in this absorbing craft.

greeting cards

chapter 1

greeting card *flowers*

I have always been fascinated by old papers, and I collect all sorts: old letters, shopping lists, maps, music, bills, tickets, stamps, postcards, wrapping paper, and even paper money. I like the patina of age and finding types of paper that are no longer available. The colors seem softer and, of course, there is always a particular history attached to each piece of paper that can set your imagination going. These scraps are perfect to use when making a small project such as this greeting card. I have used the front cover of some sheet music for the pitcher and flowers, while other scraps of printed papers were chosen for their color or pattern. The green stems were cut from the back cover of an old map of Paris.

You will need

Sharp pencil and metal ruler
9½ x 6¾in (24 x 17cm) piece of light brown or buff medium-weight cardstock
Bone scorer (a dull-edged tool used for making sharp fold lines)
Scraps of paper such as construction (sugar) paper, in dark brown and pink
Craft knife or scalpel
Cutting mat
White (PVA) glue and brush
Pattern for pitcher (see page 121)
Sheet-music front cover
Circle template ruler
Small, sharp scissors
Scraps of old printed papers in medium pink, pale pink, light brown, and green
Tracing paper
Masking tape
Origami paper in pale green

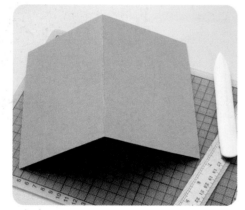

1 Measure and mark a point exactly halfway down each long side of the cardstock. Line up the ruler with these two points and score down the line between them with a bone scorer. Fold along the scored line, bending each side away from you.

2 From the dark brown paper, cut a 4¾ x 2⅛in (12 x 5.5cm) rectangle for the table using a craft knife or scalpel and a cutting mat. Give the shape a slanted top by making one of the shorter edges only 1¾in (4.5cm) deep. With the fold of the card on the left, glue the brown piece to the card front with the bottom and side edges even. From the pink paper, cut a 3¾ x 1¼in (9.5 x 3cm) rectangle for the placemat, and glue it on top of the brown table, with the lower edge along the bottom edge of the card.

Tip: *To add to the charm of the design, cut the various papers roughly by hand so that the edges are not straight. You will soon get a feel for the size or proportions that look best.*

The subtle use of faded colors, old papers, and decorative printed designs gives this card a decidedly retro look.

4 Trace the foliage in the photograph on page 13 onto tracing paper. Lay the tracing paper over a piece of green printed paper, securing it with a piece of masking tape top and bottom. Place the green paper on the cutting mat, and cut out the foliage along the traced lines, cutting through the tracing paper and the green paper at the same time.

3 Lay the pattern for the pitcher on the sheet music cover. Draw around the pattern and cut out the outer edge with the scissors. Now place it on the cutting mat and cut out the section inside the handle with a craft knife. Cut a 2 x 1³⁄₈in (5 x 3.5cm) rectangle from the medium pink printed paper and glue it on the card front ³⁄₄in (2cm) from the top, with the long right-hand edge of the rectangle even with the right edge of the card. Cut a 1¹⁄₂ x 1in (4 x 2.5cm) rectangle from the pale pink printed paper. Reversing it so that the print shows faintly through, glue it on the card front ¹⁄₄in (5mm) from the top, with the long left-hand edge of the card even with the fold.

5 On a scrap of light brown printed paper, draw an ellipse to fit at the top of the pitcher with a small amount of the rim above it, giving a three-dimensional effect. Glue it in place. Arrange the foliage pieces on top so that they appear to come out of the pitcher and spread out. Apply glue to the back of the foliage and stick in place.

6 On the sheet-music cover, use a circle template ruler to draw one 1¼in (3cm) circle, two 1⅛in (2.6cm) circles, and one 1in (2.5cm) circle; cut them out. Hold each circle in your hand over a piece of the dark brown construction (sugar) paper, and cut roughly around it with scissors so that a small uneven dark brown margin shows beneath the circles cut from the sheet-music cover. Cut out all four dark brown circles in this way.

7 Snip out eight equidistant tiny segments from the music-cover circles. Glue a dark brown circle to the end of each stem, and glue the music-cover circles centrally on top, forming the flowers. Press to make sure the glue adheres evenly.

8 For the flower stamens, cut four ⅜ x 1½in (1 x 4cm) strips of the pale green origami paper. With scissors, make close-together snips that extend two-thirds of the way across the width. Brush some glue along the uncut edge of one strip, and roll up the strip tightly so that the glue holds the roll firmly. Roll up the other three strips in the same way. When the glue is dry, press out the stamens and gently flatten. Glue a bunch of stamens into the center of each flower.

valentine card

Designing and making greeting cards is a perfect way to begin to learn the often intricate techniques of papercutting. This craft always produces a very graphic image, which is well suited to the small format of a folded card. The main motifs here are cut using a pattern, but the heart is the perfect papercutting symbol. For a symmetrical shape, it should be cut from a folded piece of paper. Any scraps of brightly colored, lightweight paper will be suitable for the motifs, but origami paper is ideal. It comes in pads of various shades, often with a contrasting color on the reverse side.

You will need

Cutting mat and metal ruler
Craft knife or scalpel
White cardstock or watercolor paper
Bone scorer (a dull-edged tool used for making sharp fold lines)
Scraps of lightweight papers, such as origami squares, in lime green, brown, pink, leaf green, yellow, and orange
White (PVA) glue and small brush
Sharp pencil
Patterns for bird, hearts, and foliage (see page 119)
Small, sharp scissors
Circle template ruler

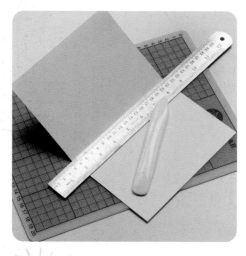

1 On the cutting mat, use the metal ruler and craft knife or scalpel to cut the white cardstock or watercolor paper into a rectangle—mine was 9 ½ x 6¾in (24 x 17cm). Mark the halfway point on both long sides, line up the ruler with the two marks, and score along the ruler with a bone scorer to create a neat folding line. Fold the piece of cardstock in half along the scored line.

2 From the lime-green paper, cut out a long, uneven rectangle measuring about 4 ½ x 1⅜in (11.5 x 3.5cm). Brush the glue evenly onto the back of the rectangle, and stick it in place on the card front along the left-hand side of the lower edge. Press to make sure the glue adheres evenly.

3 Using the sharp pencil, draw around the bird pattern on the brown paper, and cut out using the scissors. Fold a piece of pink paper in half, and place the straight side of each of the two heart patterns against the fold. Draw around the patterns with the pencil, carefully cut out, then unfold them.

4 Fold the leaf-green paper in half and place the pattern for the foliage on it (not against the fold). Draw around it, and carefully cut out the two identical pieces with the scissors.

5 Apply the glue to the back of the bird, and stick in place on top of the green rectangle, smoothing over it so that it lies completely flat.

6 Arrange the hearts and the foliage in the remaining white space, with one heart at the top of each foliage piece. When you are happy with the arrangement brush a thin layer of glue on the back of the smaller pieces and stick them in place. You don't want any glue to escape as you press the paper down.

7 Using a circle template ruler, cut two circles about 1in (2.5cm) in diameter from the yellow paper. Snip out small segments all the way around the edge of each to make them into flowers. Glue one to the center of each pink heart, applying the glue carefully so that it doesn't seep out when pressed in place.

8 Cut out three ⅜in (8mm) orange circles. Stick one in the center of each yellow flower, and use the third for the bird's eye. Draw and cut out a tail-feathers piece from orange and the bird's breast from pink, and stick them in place on top of the brown bird. Applying glue can make thin cardstock and paper misshapen, so press them flat under a heavy book to prevent this.

Tip: *If you want to introduce some pattern into the picture, you could substitute a patterned paper for one of the solid-colored ones, such as for the robin's breast.*

Although designed to be used as a change of address card, this little house framed by two trees makes a charming mantelpiece decoration. It would also be perfect as a "welcome to your new home" card, too.

change of address card

This stylish three-dimensional card is designed to be used as a change of address card, but it would also make a delightful housewarming card. Four simple folds transform the flat card into a three-dimensional house. When I had finished making it, my granddaughter wanted to use it as a dollhouse for tiny toys! Now I think I am going to have to make a whole street of houses for her to play with. I have used some small scraps of marbleized paper for the trees, some old wood-grain paper for the tree branches, and some brick-pattern paper normally used on dollhouses for the garden walls and roof tiles. To save time, you could make an original design and then make multiples by photocopying or printing it yourself.

You will need

Patterns for house and tree (see page 121)
Lightweight cardstock or stiff paper, in buff color
Sharp pencil
Cutting mat and metal ruler
Craft knife or scalpel
Scraps of marbleized paper, brick-pattern paper, and wood-grain paper
Small, sharp scissors
Pinking shears
White (PVA) glue and brush
Bone scorer (a dull-edged tool used for making sharp fold lines)

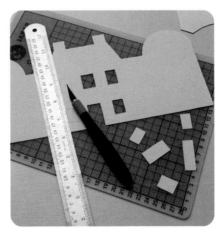

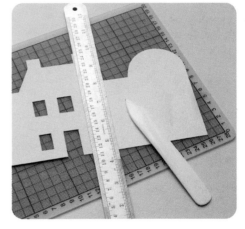

1 Place the house pattern on the cardstock or paper, and draw neatly around the pattern with a sharp pencil.

2 Put the cardstock on a cutting mat and use the ruler and the craft knife or scalpel to cut out the house and the door and windows.

3 Place the ruler along the fold lines (indicated by the dotted lines on the pattern) and score them with the bone scorer. Fold the sides of the house back along the fold lines between the sides and front of the house. Fold the outer sections (where the trees will be) forward along the fold lines between the sides and the outer sections. Fold the roof back and fold the chimneys forward along their fold lines.

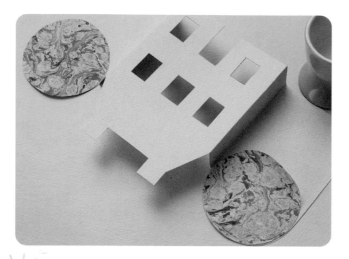

4 Cut out two 2¾in (7cm) circles from the marbleized paper. Brush glue evenly onto the backs and stick in place at the top of the outer sections.

5 Place the tree pattern on a folded piece of the wood-grain paper. Draw around the pattern and neatly cut out two trees, using either small, sharp scissors or a craft knife and cutting mat.

6 Carefully glue each tree in place on top of the marbleized circle. Press gently to smooth, making sure all parts are stuck down.

7 Cut out two 1½ x 2¾in (4 x 7cm) pieces of the brick-pattern paper to fit along the base of each tree, checking first that they will fit exactly between the outer edge and the house on each side. Glue in place. Using the house pattern, cut a roof from the brick-pattern paper, and stick in place.

8 Cut five narrow strips from the brick-pattern paper to fit on the front of the house between the windows and door (four vertically and one horizontally), and stick them in place. Cut a ¼ x 4in (7mm x 10cm) strip of marbleized paper, cutting one long edge using pinking shears. Stick in place along the bottom of the roof, with the zigzag edge at the bottom. Add a slightly wider strip of the marbleized paper at the base of the wall under each lower window, making them long enough to fit exactly between the vertical brick-paper strips flanking the windows. Finally add a dot of marbleized paper on each chimney. Reset the folds so that the house stands up independently.

Tip: *The glue can stretch the paper or card lightly as it dries, so if the cardstock warps slightly, press the finished house for a day or so under a heavy book.*

leafy postcards

Once the most common means of day-to-day communication, vintage postcards are nostalgic reminders of a time gone by. Sometimes you find a message such as "Meet me on the eight o'clock train tonight" on a card that was posted in the morning to arrive by lunchtime! Part of the charm of these vintage postcards lies in the neat, old-fashioned handwriting and plain colored stamps, so I've designed this simple project to highlight this visual quality. A papercut leaf is stuck on top of the original message, address and stamp, allowing them to partially show through, while the picture on the reverse is covered with plain paper to contain the new address, message, and stamp. You could make a number of cards at the same time, using a variety of wood-grain papers.

You will need

Cutting mat and metal ruler
Craft knife or scalpel
Scraps of wood-grain paper
Pattern for ash leaf spray (see page 124)
Pencil
Scissors (optional)
White (PVA) glue and brush
Old postcards with canceled stamps and messages, with an image on the front
Gray lightweight paper

1 With a cutting mat, metal ruler, and craft knife or scalpel, cut a 3¼ x 6in (8.5 x 15cm) piece of wood-grain paper for each postcard. Lay it wrong-side up on the cutting mat and place the pattern on top, in the center. With a pencil, draw inside the leaves and stem, and then remove the pattern. Use the craft knife to carefully cut away the parts of the leaf spray from the wood-grain paper.

2 With the scissors or craft knife, cut away a margin on each of the long sides of the wood-grain paper, checking that you will be cutting away enough to reveal part of the writing and stamp when the leaf spray shape is placed over the postcard. Brush glue onto the back, trying to cover it all, and stick it down on the postcard. Lift any unstuck points from the front and add some more glue before sticking them down firmly. Smooth gently to make sure that the paper adheres evenly. The leaf spray will protrude slightly at both ends of the postcard, so turn over the card and cut off any excess.

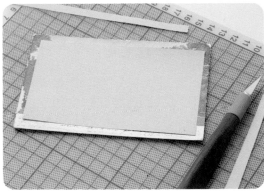

3 Turn the postcard over to reveal the picture side. Cut a 3 x 5in (8 x 13cm) piece of the gray paper, checking that it fits the picture with a margin of at least ¼in (5mm) all around.

Tip: *The craft knife or scalpel must be very sharp, especially if the paper you are using is old or in any way delicate. In fact, a sharp craft knife is safer to use than a dull one.*

4 Stick the gray paper in place and smooth over it to make sure that the glue adheres evenly. Cut an uneven ¼ x 2¾in (5mm x 7cm) strip of wood-grain paper. Stick it vertically across the paper to mark the division between the space for the address and the space for the message.

wedding key gift tag

These elegant gift tags could be used on wedding favors given to guests or on the pretty boxes in which the cake is sometimes distributed, or they could be used on wedding presents. A symbol traditionally associated with marriage, the key motif probably represents the "key" to a new life. It is an interesting form, and you can either use the pattern provided or design your own key shape to go inside the oval frames with scalloped edges. The directions are for making two gift tags, in reversed colors. If you know the couple's wedding color scheme, you could choose cardstock to match instead of using the colors shown here.

You will need

Patterns for frame and key
  (see page 119)
One 7in (18cm) square of lightweight
  cardstock in each of two colors,
  such as pink and white
Sharp pencil
Small, sharp scissors
Craft knife or scalpel
Cutting mat
Small hole punch
White (PVA) glue and brush

1 Place the frame pattern on the pink cardstock square and draw around it twice with a pencil. On one of the ovals also draw the inner oval, but don't draw it on the other oval. Repeat on the white cardstock square.

2 Carefully cut around the outer pencil lines with the scissors, then use a craft knife or scalpel and a cutting mat to cut out the inner oval from one pink and one white oval. These will be the frame fronts, and the ovals without the cut-out centers will be the frame backs.

Tip: *Choose a pretty pink silk ribbon at least ³⁄₈in (1cm) wide to attach the gift tag to the favor, cake box, or wedding present.*

3 Lay the key pattern on the remaining scraps of pink and white cardstock and draw around it once on each color. Cut out the two keys using the scissors, plus the craft knife and cutting mat for the tricky areas and to remove the inside "ring" at the top of the key.

4 Use the hole punch to make holes in each of the scallops around the two frame fronts, omitting the larger scallop at the top. Brush glue onto the back of the white frame front and stick it onto the pink frame back. Make a hole for attaching the tag in the double layer at the top. Stick the pink frame front to the white frame back in the same way.

5 Brush the glue carefully on the back of the white key (so it doesn't ooze out when you press the key in place) and stick it to the center of the pink frame back. Stick the pink key to the white frame back in the same way.

 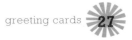

easter rabbit *gift tag*

This cute little Easter bunny gift tag is perfect for tying to the handle of a small basket that is used to collect Easter eggs. Carefully hiding Easter eggs among the early flowers in the garden on Easter Sunday is a tradition in our house. If you have a number of children or grandchildren, or their friends are visiting, you could write each child's name on the back of the gift tag so that they can all identify their own collecting basket.

You will need

3in (8cm) square of medium-weight laid paper (this has a faint ribbed texture) in blue-gray
Cutting mat
Patterns for rabbit and oval (see page 118)
Sharp pencil and ruler
Craft knife or scalpel
4in (10cm) square of medium-weight cardstock in duck-egg blue
4in (10cm) square of lightweight handmade paper (this has a textured, slightly uneven surface) in brown
Small, sharp scissors
Pinking shears
White (PVA) glue and brush
Small hole punch

1 Place the laid paper on the cutting mat, lay the rabbit pattern on it, and draw around the pattern carefully with the pencil. Cut it out with a craft knife or scalpel. Mark the eye through the hole in the pattern. Remove the pattern and, referring to it, draw fine lines representing the legs, tail, and ears, then cut small slits along the pencil lines using the craft knife.

2 Place the oval pattern on the blue cardstock and draw around it. Repeat for the brown paper. Carefully cut out both ovals using the small scissors. Now draw a line ⅛in (4mm) inside the brown oval all the way around and cut along it with the pinking shears.

3 Punch a hole in the paper rabbit for the eye. Brush glue sparingly on the back of the rabbit (don't use too much or the glue might seep through the slits) and stick it in the center of the brown oval. Press to make sure that the glue adheres evenly.

4 Apply glue evenly to the back of the brown oval, and press in place in the center of the blue oval, taking care that the blue margin is as even as possible all the way around. When dry, punch a hole at the top and press the rabbit flat under a heavy book.

Tip: *Make a number of similar tags but vary the colors. You can use soft, gentle colors, but remember that if the rabbit is light-colored you will need a contrasting background so that the rabbit will stand out.*

This lovely envelope, with its elegant gloved hand, makes an ideal cover for a special or significant invitation.

decorated envelope

This stylish papercut of a hand holding a card is designed to be stuck to the front of a plain envelope, transforming an everyday item into something special. It may even impress your mail carrier as it will certainly stand out from the bundle of utilitarian letters that must be delivered each day. Using a pattern, it is quick and easy to make. Although you would probably only use this decoration for significant or celebratory cards and letters, you could photocopy the front of your decorated envelope for use on other envelopes.

You will need

Pattern for hand with card
  (see page 125)
White cartridge paper
Sharp pencil and eraser
Scissors
Cutting mat and craft knife or scalpel
Bookbinder's paste (50 percent PVA)
  and brush
Scrap of thin printing paper (optional)

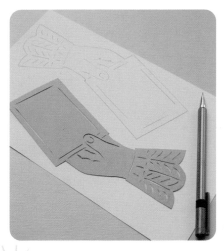

1 Lay the pattern on the paper and draw around it with a sharp pencil. Also mark through the narrow lines. Because these internal lines are so narrow, you will not be able to clearly mark them. Therefore, when you remove the pattern, draw in any portions of the lines that have failed to register through the slits.

Tip: *You could reverse the effect by cutting the hand from dark or colored paper before attaching it to a light-colored envelope.*

2 With the scissors, cut out the hand holding a card, then use a craft knife or scalpel to cut narrow slits where marked. These cut lines should start and end together, opening out only slightly along the length. Look at the photograph of the finished project to see how neatly these lines are cut. When you become more experienced with a craft knife or scalpel, you almost feel that you are "drawing" with the blade.

4 Lift the paper shape, turn it over, and hold it over the envelope front so that you can be sure of the right position. Lay it down and swiftly smooth the surface (you can do this through a thin piece of printing paper if you wish) to remove any wrinkles or bubbles.

3 Apply the paste evenly to the back of the paper shape, making sure that the paste does not show through the cut lines. Using bookbinder's paste means that you have a little time to work before the paste dries.

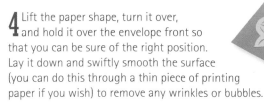

cut-out envelope *monograms*

With the development of the Internet not so many letters are written today, so it is always a welcome surprise to receive a handwritten letter. This stylish project is a simple, modern way to make your envelopes more personal, by using a single letter as a monogram (either your own initial or the recipient's). The letter pictured here, which I traced from one in my collection of typefaces, has been cut through the front of the envelope. This decorative technique will reveal the paper inside without giving away any of its secrets. A set of such envelopes would make a lovely gift.

You will need

Small, sharp scissors
Ruler and sharp pencil
Scrap of an old map (see advice about using old maps on page 44)
White (PVA) glue and brush
Business-size envelope such as one measuring 8½ x 4¼in (22 x 11cm), in pale green or a color of your choice
Letter to use as a pattern (see Tip)
Cutting mat
Craft knife or scalpel with a new, sharp blade
Scrap of thick cardboard to fit into envelope
Scrap of light-colored paper

1 Using scissors, roughly cut out a 2 x 2¾in (5 x 7cm) rectangle from the map scrap—don't cut it out too exactly, as it should appear to have been cut "by eye." Brush glue onto the back. Stick it to the front of the envelope at bottom left, with the longer sides parallel to the base and leaving a ½in (12mm) margin at the left and bottom. Allow the glue to dry.

2 Find or print out a letter (see Tip) that is 1¼in (3cm) tall. Using a cutting mat and a craft knife or scalpel, cut out the letter to make a pattern. Lay this on the map rectangle, just left of the center. Draw around the letter shape.

3 Remove the pattern and insert the cardboard into the envelope on the left side so it is beneath the letter. It may be difficult to see the pencil lines on the heavily patterned map, so work in a good light. Cut out the letter very carefully.

4 Remove the cut-away letter and the cardboard, and insert a light-colored piece of paper in order to fully reveal the cut-out shape. Check that the edges of the letter are cut neatly. If you need to make any adjustments, insert the cardboard once more before attempting to make any corrections with the knife. Remove the light-colored paper. When you eventually use the envelope, make sure the paper you put inside is a light color so that the cut-out initial shows up clearly.

Tip: *Interesting typefaces are all around—in newspapers, magazines, and packaging—so cut out and collect any that appeal. You could also download fonts from the computer, enlarge them to the correct size, and then print them out.*

party decorations
chapter 2

paper bag *lanterns*

This is a really simple project that is transformed into something impressive when lit up at night. Each lantern is decorated with two moths—the one that shines brightly has been cut out of the bag, while the darker one is simply the cut-out moth stuck onto the bag. Illuminated by a flickering candle flame (safely contained within a glass jar), these two night visitors look as if they have been attracted to the light and have landed on the bag. The lanterns are made from block-bottomed bags—the type used as brown grocery sacks or as flour bags. You can find colored or patterned ones in gift stores. If feeling adventurous, you may want to construct your own bag with a special paper. Just unfold and take apart a store-bought bag and recreate it using your own paper.

You will need

Patterned block-bottomed paper bags
Piece of cardboard (the back of a stiff brown envelope will do), cut to fit loosely inside the bag
Pattern for moth (see page 125)
Sharp pencil and eraser
Craft knife or scalpel
White (PVA) glue and small brush
Glass jars and votive candles

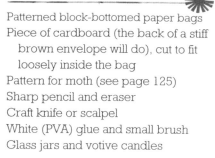

1 Lay each bag flat, and put the piece of cardboard inside. Place the moth pattern on the bag at a slight angle, 1½in (4cm) from the top. Holding the pattern in place, draw around it carefully using a sharp pencil.

2 Remove the pattern and use a craft knife or scalpel to cut around the moth shape, taking particular care around the narrow parts of the antennae.

3 Place the cut-out moth on the lower half of the bag so that it leans in the opposite direction to the upper moth. Mark the position in pencil. Brush glue onto the back of the moth and stick it in place on the bag.

Tip: *If you attach the lower moth to the bag loosely, gluing only parts of the wings rather than the whole moth, this will give the impression that the moth has just landed on the glowing lantern.*

4 Lightly draw a number of eight-pointed stars (made up of four equidistant crossed lines) around the bag using the pencil. Cut along these lines so that you cut through the paper, then gently erase the pencil lines. Don't worry too much if a few lines remain, as these will not show when the lanterns are illuminated. Remove the cardboard and open up the base of the bag so that it stands up. Put a votive in each glass jar, light them, and carefully place one inside each bag.

snowflake *christmas crackers*

Making a snowflake is one of those magical folding and cutting exercises that we all learn as children. The classic technique never fails to charm and surprise, as you don't really know what design will emerge until you open up the folded circle. There are so many ways that this technique can be used. I have designed these pretty Christmas cracker party favors with a colorful snowflake added to the front of each. Christmas crackers can be expensive to buy, but they are really easy to make, as they basically consist of just decorated cardboard tubes containing a tiny gift, a snapper to make the pop, and a decorated paper hat (see page 42). The instructions are for one cracker but you will probably want to make a set.

(see page 42)

You will need

Sharp pencil
Three cardboard tubes, such as toilet paper tubes, about 4in (10cm) long
Lightweight patterned papers, cut into one 7½ x 12in (19 x 30cm) piece for each
White (PVA) glue and brush
Double-sided tape
Two 10in (25cm) silk ribbons for each cracker
Scissors
Lightweight, flexible paper such as origami paper, in a different color for each cracker
Cutting mat and craft knife or scalpel (optional)
Pattern for snowflake (see page 120)

Pattern for snowflake (see page 120)

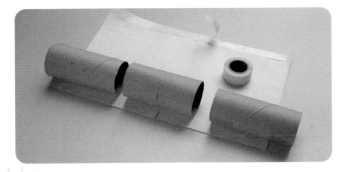

1 With a pencil, mark the center of one tube, and the center of the long edge of a piece of patterned paper on the wrong side. Glue the tube to the paper at the edge, matching the marks. Stick double-sided tape along the opposite edge. Place the other two tubes at either end, but do not stick them down.

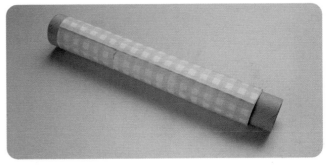

2 Carefully roll the central tube over the paper, so that the entire piece of paper rolls up into a long tube around the three cardboard tubes. Stick the taped edge neatly in place where it meets the right side of the other edge.

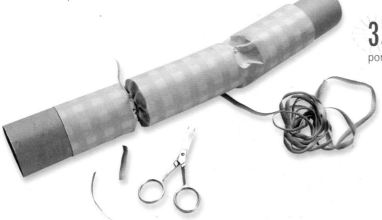

3 Press the paper in slightly at one end of the central tube, and tie a ribbon around this portion, pulling it in against the end of the tube. Do the same at the other end of the central tube in the same way. Trim off the ends of the ribbons with scissors. Remove the outer tubes.

4 Using the scissors, cut the origami paper into 3in (8cm) squares, one for each cracker. Fold each square in half along the diagonal, then in half again, so that there are four layers forming a triangle that measures 3in (8cm) along the bottom edge. Fold the top double-layer triangle in half by folding it back on itself. Do the same to the remaining double-layer triangle. You now have a triangle eight layers thick.

5 Mark 1½in (4cm) down the long side to match the other side in length, and draw an arc from the mark to the opposite point of the triangle.

6 With the scissors, cut along the arc through all eight layers, and discard the small portion you have cut away.

7 Use the snowflake pattern to draw a design on the folded-paper (or devise your own if you prefer).

Tip: *Folding the square as explained in step 4 gives eight folds in alternating directions. This makes the folded square easier to cut through in step 8 than if you just folded it in half four times.*

8 Cut away the marked parts using either scissors or, for a neater finish, a craft knife or scalpel with a cutting mat.

9 Open out the snowflake and press flat with your hand. Apply a small amount of glue to the center of the back and press it in place at the center of the cracker.

christmas *party hat*

This pretty pink striped party hat is made from a soft, rather flexible handmade decorative paper. It is much more durable than the traditional tissue-paper hat found in Christmas crackers. As the paper is flexible, you could fold this hat and insert it into the center of your homemade cracker (see page 38), and then add a tiny gift to create a genuine surprise when the cracker is pulled. The pink tissue trim along the base of the hat reminds me of the decorative band that we always fixed around our homemade Christmas cake. To decorate the hat for a children's party, you could add a few stick-on jewels, along the center of the pink tissue trim around the base. The hat is simple enough to make that it won't take you long to produce a set of party hats for everyone at the event.

You will need

Eggcup, 2⅛in (5.5cm) in diameter
4¾ x 22in (12 x 56cm) piece of
  medium-weight rag paper
  (a fibrous decorative paper) in
  pink stripe
Sharp pencil
Cutting mat
Craft knife or scalpel
Flower pattern (see page 120)
Two 2 x 22in (5 x 56cm) strips of
  lightweight tissue-type rag paper
  in pink
Small, sharp scissors
White (PVA) glue and brush
Small hole punch
Two decorative paper fasteners,
  in pink or orange

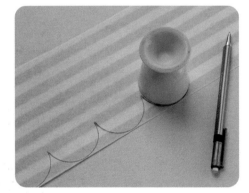

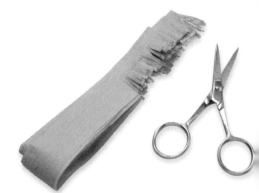

1 Stand the eggcup upside down at one long edge of the striped paper, and draw around half of it with a pencil. Now move it along the edge so that the side of the eggcup touches the previously drawn line, and draw around it again. Repeat this all along one side. At the end there won't be room for a whole scallop, so draw a straight line parallel to the edge and even with the points of the scallops.

2 Place the striped paper on a cutting mat and use a craft knife or scalpel to cut along the scalloped line. At the end where you drew a straight line, cut along that line. Lay the flower pattern on each scallop and mark the petals with the pencil through the holes in the pattern. With the paper still on the cutting mat, use the craft knife to cut out each of the flower petals.

3 Lay one tissue-paper strip on top of the other, and fold them in half lengthwise. Fold in half crosswise, and then in half crosswise again, so the folded strips are now 16 layers thick and about 5½in (14cm) long. Using small, sharp scissors, make cuts a scant ⅛in (2–3mm) apart and ¾in (2cm) long, along the cut edge (not the folded edge as in some other projects).

4 Unfold the strips and pull them gently apart. Brush a line of glue ⅜ in (1cm) wide onto the lower edge of the striped paper, ⅜ in (1cm) away from the edge. Lay one of the tissue strips along this line of glue, making sure that only the central, uncut section touches the glue. Press into place. Add some more glue along the center of this tissue strip and stick the other strip on top in the same manner.

5 Bring the two ends together so the scalloped end overlaps the end with the straight cut-away top. Holding the two ends together, use the hole punch to make a small hole through both layers ¾ in (2cm) from the base. Push a paper fastener into the hole and open out the wings on the inside. Punch a hole near the top edge of the overlapping piece ⅝ in (1.5cm) below the flower. Mark through this hole onto the piece beneath, punch a hole in this lower section, and join the two pieces with a second paper fastener.

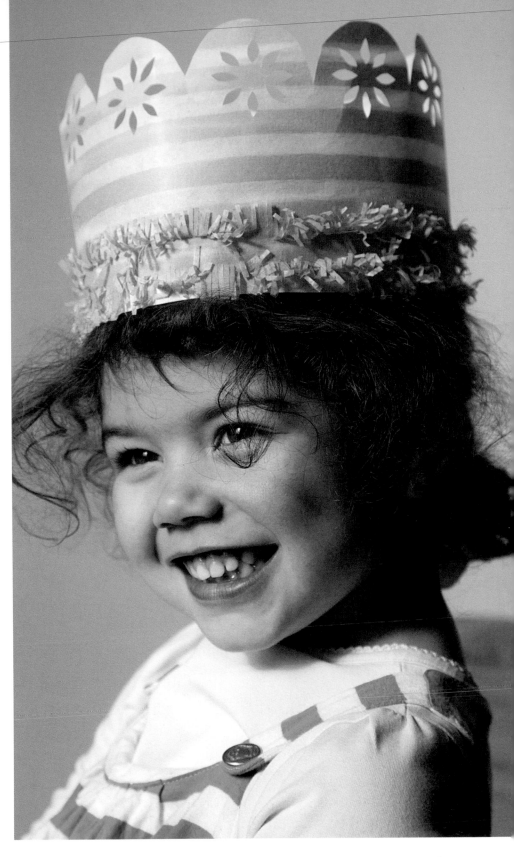

Tip: *You could reinforce the two ends of the hat with strips of the same paper stuck on the inside. This makes the hat more durable and it is also easier to punch the holes.*

contour map starbursts

Maps are wonderful—they are colorful, beautiful, historical, and informative. They are also printed on very large sheets of lightweight paper, which makes them ideal for papercuts, especially in projects like this one involving a lot of folds. Although antique maps are too valuable to use for this, most people have a collection of maps that they may be happy to part with. Specialist map shops are another possible source, as they discard maps that become out of date. I've used contour maps here because they often contain large areas of different colors, which look dramatic once the paper is pleated for the starbursts. The instructions are for making one starburst.

You will need

Colorful map
Scissors
Ruler and sharp pencil
Cutting mat and craft knife or scalpel
Pattern for starburst (see page 123)
Double-sided tape
White (PVA) glue and glue brush

Tip: *You could insert a string or hanging thread between the two ends, at the outside edge, before it is stuck together in a circle.*

1 Cut the map into 4¼ x 36in (11 x 90cm) strips, one for each starburst. Mark a line across the strip ¾in (2cm) from one end. Fold the paper over carefully along that line.

2 Fold the strip into ¾in (2cm) pleats by repeatedly turning the paper over and folding, so that the new fold you are making is always facing you. This is the best way of keeping the folds as even as possible. Keep folding until the paper is all used up. If the short edges at the sides are at all uneven, place on a cutting mat and trim neatly with a craft knife or scalpel.

3 Lay the pattern on the pleated paper, with the straight side of the pattern against the unfolded edge of the pleated paper. Draw around the pattern.

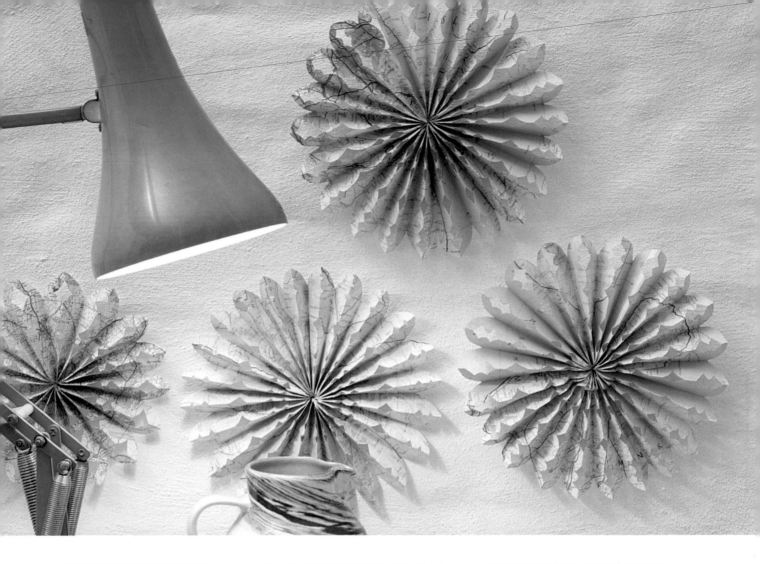

4 Using a cutting mat and the craft knife, cut away the small parts that you have drawn on the pleated paper. The layers will not all come away at once, so you will need to cut slowly and carefully through all of them.

5 Open up the paper from one side and bring it around into a circle. Use the double-sided tape to join the sides from each end. This can be tricky, so be patient.

6 Lay the starburst on a piece of paper and drip some glue into the center so that the folds are held firmly and neatly together. Allow the glue to set.

room garland

This cheerful garland is easy to make and is a lovely project to do with children. The design is based on the classic papercutting technique of folding and cutting paper to create a repetitive design—similar to the old favorite, the ubiquitous snowflake that we all learned to make at school. The simple cutting pattern used here is inspired by a sunrise, a well-known art deco motif. I have used a selection of origami paper squares, which are thin and flexible enough for folding. They come in many colors and in various sizes, some with a different color on each side. For this project you can use double- or single-sided paper, or a combination of both.

You will need

6in (15cm) origami squares in assorted solid colors—you need two contrasting squares per papercut
Sunrise pattern (see page 118)
Sharp pencil
Cutting mat
Craft knife or scalpel
White (PVA) glue and brush
Scissors
Thin string, in a color to match garland

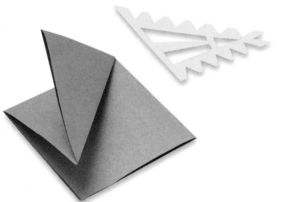

1 Fold a square of origami paper in half, then fold it in half again, making a 1½in (3.75cm) square. Fold the top two layers together, back on themselves along the diagonal. Turn over and fold the other two layers back in the same way and along the same diagonal. Folding the paper in this way makes it less bulky and the cuts more accurate than with conventional folding.

2 Lay the sunrise pattern on the folded paper, matching the V-shaped cut to the central corner (where there are only folds and no outside edges). Draw around the pattern with a pencil. Remove the pattern and place the folded paper on a cutting mat. Cut away the marked areas with a craft knife or scalpel. You will be cutting through eight layers, so you may have to unfold the paper to cut away the lower layers. However, if your craft knife is sharp, this should not be necessary.

Tip: *To make a garland that can be viewed from each side, glue a second papercut to the back.*

3 Gently unfold the paper to reveal the cut-out design, but don't flatten it. Take a different-colored square of origami paper and use the point of the brush to put a small dab of glue in each corner and in the center of each side, at the edge, applying it sparingly.

4 Lower the cut-out square over the uncut square onto the blobs of glue, being careful to make the edges of the squares even. Press down the cut-out piece over these blobs of glue so that the two layers are held together only at these points. This will produce a three-dimensional effect with interesting shadows. Make the remaining papercuts in the same way until you have enough for the whole garland, ready to string together.

5 Brush glue on the back of a square along the top edge only. Lay the string along the line of glue, leaving extra string at the end for attaching. To hold the string taut, place a heavy object on each end. Cut one ⅝ x 6in (1.5 x 15cm) strip of origami paper for each papercut, in the same color as the back of the square. Lay a strip over the string and press, so the glue holds the string in place. Leave 2¼in (6cm) of bare string then add the next square. Continue in this way, leaving extra at the end for attaching.

winter reindeer

A satisfying project to make, these wintry-looking reindeer are designed to stand together in a small herd. This is a simple way of creating a three-dimensional object from flat elements. The body is bent over after the head and tail have been attached, so that the reindeer stands. It wouldn't stand indefinitely, however, as the paper has a memory and would gradually open out once more. Therefore the little saddle is not only decorative but functional—its girth holds the body and legs in the standing position.

You will need

Patterns for reindeer head, tail, body, and saddle (see page 124)
Lightweight cardstock in Wedgwood blue, with white on reverse—an 8 x 6in (20 x 15cm) piece is enough for two reindeer
Sharp pencil
Cutting mat and craft knife or scalpel
White (PVA) glue and brush
Large knitting needle
4 x 3in (10 x 8cm) piece of laid paper, with a faint stripe in the texture—I used one in dark blue
Small, sharp scissors
Two hole punches, one small and one large

Tip: *You could use the same technique to make other animals, such as squirrels, foxes, or bears. Look at some images for reference and then simplify the shape before separating it into the constituent parts of head, tail, and body.*

1 Draw around the patterns for the reindeer head, tail, and body on the cardstock with a pencil, once for each reindeer. Remove the patterns and, referring to the patterns, mark where the slits are to be cut. For a reindeer that faces in the other direction, just turn the head and tail over. Cut out using a craft knife or scalpel and cutting mat. Cut the slits along the marked lines. Check they are correct by holding the portions that will be slotted through them (the base of the head and of the tail) against the slits.

2 Push the base of the head piece through the slit at the front of the body, and push the base of the tail through the slit at the back. Cut two ¼ x ⅝in (5 x 15mm) pieces of cardstock. Turn the body over and push one of these small pieces through the slit in the part of the head piece that protrudes onto the underside of the body. Dab glue behind the small piece on either side of the protruding neck, holding it in place until the glue dries. Repeat for the other small piece and the tail.

3 Turn the reindeer right side up, and bend the body over the knitting needle to help curve the back, which brings the legs into a standing position. Place the saddle pattern on the laid paper, draw around it, and cut out the saddle with small, sharp scissors.

4 Fold the wider portion of the saddle piece in half crosswise, and use hole punches to make a flower shape through both layers by punching a large hole in the center surrounded by smaller holes. (Temporarily inserting a scrap of cardstock between the two halves of the folded saddle while you punch the holes, then removing it, will produce neater holes.) Unfold the saddle piece.

5 Apply the glue to the back of the wider portion but not to the girth (the narrow portion). Stick the saddle on the reindeer's back, and bring the girth under the body, pulling the two sides together. Check it is tight enough, and cut away a small piece at the end of the girth so it meets the saddle without overlapping. Using a dab of glue on the tip of the girth, glue the girth to the horse.

6 Use the small hole punch to make a hole for the reindeer's eye, which should be in line with the front of the ear. (As in step 4, temporarily place a scrap of cardstock behind the area to be punched to make a neater hole.)

gifts & treats

chapter 3

three-dimensional daffodils

Paper sculpture, folding, and cutting are closely related, and here is a project that employs all three techniques. Although the project is somewhat intricate, each stage is simple and the resulting daffodils are surprisingly lifelike. The three-dimensional effect of the petals and the central trumpet is achieved by simply cutting a slit and then overlapping the sides slightly before sticking them back together. A delicate yellow tissue paper has been glued to a plain drawing paper and this two-sided effect is very striking. You may like to try making other types of flowers—those with a limited number of petals are most suitable. Snowdrops, for example, would work really well.

You will need

Yellow tissue paper
White lightweight cartridge paper or
  other drawing paper
Large scissors
Spray glue suitable for repositioning
Patterns for petal and trumpet
  (see page 120)
Sharp pencil
Small, sharp scissors
White (PVA) glue and brush
Small pair of long-nosed pliers
Strong paper-covered florist's wires,
  each 8–10in (20–25cm) long
Knitting needle

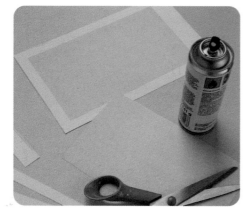

1 You can make two flowers from a 9 x 6in (23 x 15cm) rectangle of yellow tissue paper, and the same of white cartridge paper, so, using large scissors, cut out the amount you need for the number of daffodils you are making. Working outdoors or in a well-ventilated space, spray the front of the white cartridge paper liberally with the spray glue. Allow a few seconds for the glue to become sticky, and then carefully lay the yellow tissue paper on it. Smooth it out with your hands to make sure that the glue adheres evenly.

2 Turn this rectangle over so that the white side is facing upward. Lay the patterns on the paper, draw around them with a pencil, and cut out with small, sharp scissors. For each flower you will need five petals and one trumpet piece, plus one 1 x 2¾in (2.5 x 7cm) rectangle for the stamens.

3 With the small scissors, cut a slit through the center of each petal, along the central line. Working on the white side, brush white (PVA) glue along one side of the split, then bring the other side slightly over the split onto the glue, so that the overlap creates the curve in the petal. Hold the two sides together until the glue has set enough to hold itself. Repeat for the other petals.

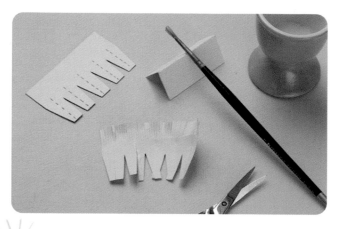

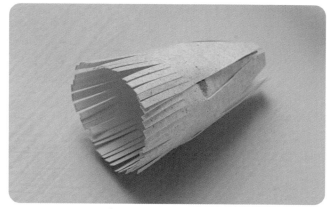

4 Along the long, uncut edge of the trumpet piece, cut snips ⅝in (1.5cm) long and very close together. Cut a slit partway down the center of each of the five sections on the opposite edge of the trumpet piece, as indicated by the dotted lines in the photograph above. Glue and overlap each of these five sections in the same way as for the petals (step 3).

5 Roll up the trumpet into a tube and glue together along the join—it helps to put one finger into the tube and hold another against it along the seam while the glue dries.

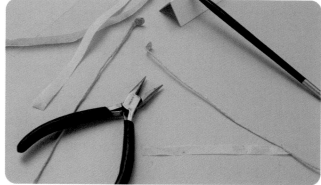

6 Using small strips of tissue paper with glue brushed onto them, bind around the base of the trumpet to draw in the separate elements and produce the trumpet shape. This can be a delicate job, but when the glue dries it looks very neat. You could also paste short pieces of tissue along the seams. Place a good dab of glue on the base of the white interior of the petal. Press the petal against the lower part of the trumpet. Stick the remaining four petals to the trumpet in the same way, positioning them so they are equidistant. While the glue is drying, place the flower upside down on a paintbrush handle or pencil end, to keep the petals in the right place.

7 Hold one end of the florist's wire in the pliers and bend it into a tight spiral about ¼in (5mm) across, then bend the spiral at right angles to the rest of the wire, which will form the flower stem. Cut two or three strips of the tissue paper, each ⅜in (1cm) wide and about 8in (20cm) long (or the length of the sheet of tissue). Apply glue to one side, and then bind the stem with one strip at a time, starting at the base and wrapping the tissue paper tightly but gently around the wire. Wind the tissue paper tightly around the spiral at the top end.

8 Dab glue into the base of the trumpet. Insert the stem and thread it through to the other side, pulling firmly so the spiral anchors it. Allow the glue to dry for 10 minutes. Neatly bind the bottom of the flower with two or three more glued strips of tissue, as in step 7, wrapping them around the base of the petals and to the top of the stem. Make the stamens by snipping three-quarters of the way across the width of the stamen piece along one long edge, then gluing along the uncut long edge and rolling it up, yellow side inward. Dab glue into the base of the trumpet and then insert the roll. When the glue has dried, open out the stamens with a knitting needle.

Tip: *Because the tissue paper is so fine, you can press it firmly against the flower when binding its base with glued strips in step 8, to iron out any crinkles or folds as the glue dries.*

lovebird decoration

This pretty decoration is designed to hang in a window, but it could also be used as a mobile over a baby's crib. The little pink bird moves freely within the heart and so is double-sided. The heart shape itself is a classic papercutting motif, since folding a paper once and then cutting a half-heart on the fold is a foolproof way of guaranteeing symmetry. Because a thick cartridge paper is used here, it will be necessary to cut out most of the elements with a craft knife or scalpel.

You will need

Sharp pencil and ruler
6 ¼ x 8in (16 x 20cm) piece of thick white cartridge paper
Bone scorer (a dull-edged tool used for making sharp fold lines)
Patterns for heart, bird, and heart backing (see page 118)
Cutting mat
Craft knife or scalpel
4in (10cm) square of lightweight pink cardstock
Small hole punch
8in (20cm) square of lightweight green cardstock
White (PVA) glue and brush
Small, sharp scissors
1yd (1m) of ⅛in- (4mm-) wide silk ribbon in pale pink

1 Measure and mark the midpoint on both short edges of the white paper rectangle. Place a ruler across these points and score a fold line using the bone scorer. Fold the paper in half along the scored line. Now place the half-heart pattern on the folded paper with its straight side along the fold. Draw around the pattern and then remove it.

2 Using a cutting mat and a craft knife or scalpel, cut out the white heart carefully. It is best to cut just inside the lines, otherwise the shape will be too large and you will be left with pencil lines to erase. Be careful with this, as you will be pressing the knife quite firmly so that it cuts through the two layers. Cut away the internal areas, taking care to make smooth lines. Think of the process as "drawing" with the knife.

This delicate heart motif, with a lovebird center and made in subtle colors, hangs from the brass handle of an old closet door. The lovebird, used on its own, would also make a pretty gift tag.

Tip: *You could make and hang together a number of hearts, each surrounding a separate motif, such as a flower, a bell, a bow, a teddy bear—the choice is yours.*

3 Draw around the bird pattern twice on the pink cardstock. Referring to the pattern, copy the fine lines onto the two birds—two across the neck, three along the wing, and two following the shape of the tail on each bird. Use the craft knife to cut these narrow slits, each of which should be widest at the center. Now cut around the outline of each bird, and use the hole punch to make an eye on each head.

4 Lay the pattern for the heart backing on the green cardstock, and draw around it. Cut it out neatly using the craft knife, but this time don't cut inside the pencil lines or you might make it too small. Take care cutting out the internal shapes, especially the small heart at the top.

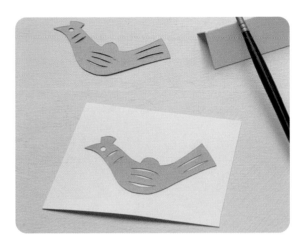

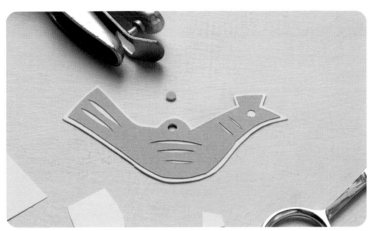

5 Brush glue onto the back of one of the pink birds, being careful not to use too much glue, which could seep through the tiny slits in the bird. Stick the bird to the remaining white cartridge paper.

6 Use small, sharp scissors to cut around the outside of the pink bird, leaving a scant ⅛in (3mm) margin of white showing all around. Turn the mounted bird over and glue the other pink bird to the white side, leaving a similar white margin all around. Use the hole punch to make a hole in the small tab at the top of the bird's back.

7 Apply glue to the back of the white paper heart that you made in steps 1–2. Lower it carefully onto the green heart backing, making sure that there will be an even margin of green all the way around. Press into place, carefully smoothing it so the glue adheres evenly. With the hole punch, make two holes, one at the very top and one in the circle at top center of the larger heart.

8 Cut a 4in (10cm) length of ribbon, and thread it through the hole at the top of the bird and then through the hole at the top of the larger heart. Tie the ends in a double knot at the back (on the green side) and cut off to leave ends ⅝in (1.5cm) long. Thread the remaining ribbon through the hole at the top and use this to hang the decoration in the window.

gardener's notebook

This lovely notebook is very simple to make. The design appears as a shape cut out of a piece of hand-blocked patterned wallpaper that is pasted onto a plain notebook, the spine of which has been covered with pink construction (sugar) paper. I collect all sorts of papers—patterned, plain, and textured—in the same way that I collect fabrics to use in patchwork or appliqué projects. Old wallpaper designs are fabulous and if you can get hold of any wallpaper sample books (the hand-blocked varieties are best), you will have a wealth of colors and designs to work with.

You will need

Notebook—mine was 6¾in (17cm) square
Pink construction (sugar) paper
Cutting mat and metal ruler
Craft knife or scalpel
Bookbinder's paste (50 percent PVA glue) and brush
Piece of hand-blocked floral wallpaper
Pattern for bird (see page 120)
Scrap of lime-green paper
Sharp pencil and eraser
Small, sharp scissors (optional)
Scrap of white paper (optional)

1 Place the pink paper on a cutting mat and, using a metal ruler and a craft knife or scalpel, cut it to size, so that it will cover the front and will wrap around the spine of the book to cover about 1½in (4cm) of the back, with the edges even. I cut mine to 8¾ x 6¾in (22 x 17cm). Brush the paste onto the front of the book up to the spine, lay the paper over the pasted cover, lining up the right-hand edges, and smooth it down. Turn the book over and bend or fold the paper around the spine partway onto the back. Mark where it reaches to and apply paste to the spine and the back as far as this mark. Firmly press the paper around the spine, making sure that both surfaces have complete contact with each other.

2 From portions of your wallpaper that do not have large motifs, cut out two pieces, each the size of the front cover excluding ¾in (2cm) of the spine—I cut mine to 6in (15cm) wide x 7in (17cm) deep.

3 For the front, lay the bird pattern in the center of one wallpaper piece. Cut a 1½ x 3¼in (4 x 8.5cm) rectangle from the lime-green scrap. Place it below the bird, so the bird appears to be standing on it, leaving a gap of ⅝in (1.5cm) between the bottom edge of the rectangle and the base of the book. Mark the position of the rectangle and then remove it. Draw around the bird using a sharp pencil.

Tip: *Because the wallpaper is cut flush with the edges of the notebook, it's important for the edges of the wallpaper to be securely stuck down, so make sure you apply the paste thinly right up to the edges.*

4 Remove the pattern and then, using the cutting mat, cut out the bird shape with the craft knife or scalpel. You can use scissors but the sharp, precise blade of the craft knife or scalpel makes you less likely to damage the wallpaper.

5 Brush paste onto the back of the wallpaper and stick it onto the front of the book, with the edges even. Press down to make sure the paste adheres well, if necessary covering the delicate wallpaper with a scrap of white paper as you press to avoid marking the wallpaper.

6 Apply paste to the back of the rectangle and stick it in place below the bird's feet. Press to secure. When the paste is dry, rub away any pencil lines with an eraser.

7 Turn the book over, and paste the second piece of wallpaper to the back as in step 5. There should be a ¾in (2cm) margin of pink paper showing at the spine. Press to make sure the glue adheres, protecting the delicate wallpaper surface with white paper, as in step 5. Place a heavy book on top of the covered notebook and leave until the paste has dried, to make sure that the new covers dry flat.

decorated eggs

This a lovely, simple project to make. An egg is the most perfect form to work with, so when you decorate it, be aware that anything you add should enhance rather than confuse the beautiful form. After all, the shape is the major part of your design. Here, decorative bands of pink and blue paper divide the egg into perfect quarter sections, each decorated with an identical leaf motif. It is important to use soft, flexible paper, as it has to fit around the curve of the egg. Even though the glue will soften the paper somewhat, a lightweight recycled paper will work best. I have used a lightweight construction (sugar) paper. The instructions are for one egg, but you could decorate a number, in different colors.

You will need

Ruler and sharp pencil
Lightweight recycled paper in pink and pale blue
Pinking shears
Large scissors
Blown egg (see Tip)
White (PVA) glue and brush
Leaf pattern (see page 121)
Small, sharp scissors
Large hole punch

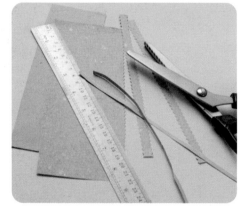

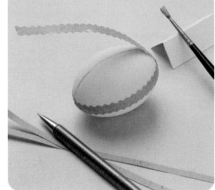

2 With the pencil, draw two lines running lengthwise all the way around the egg, dividing it into quarters. Brush glue onto the back of one pink strip. Starting at one end, stick it down one side of the egg and up the other, covering the pencil line. When you get back to the starting point, cut off the excess before sticking the end of the strip down. Wrap the second pink strip around the egg to cover the other pencil line; this strip will cross over the previous one at the ends.

1 For each egg, use a ruler and pencil to measure and mark out two 8 x ½in (20cm x 12mm) pink strips, and carefully cut them out using pinking shears. Now use large scissors to cut out two 8 x ¼in (20 x 5mm) blue strips, cutting these narrow strips without measuring, to add to the handmade look.

3 In the same way, stick the two blue strips around the egg on top of the pink strips.

Tip: *For this project to last, you need to use blown eggs (eggshells that have been drained of their contents). To blow an egg, poke a hole in each end of a room-temperature egg using a large sewing needle. Enlarge one hole and hold it over a bowl while you blow gently through the small hole. Rinse and drain.*

4 Place the leaf pattern on a small piece of the pale blue paper and draw around it with a pencil. Remove the pattern and use small, sharp scissors to cut out the shape and snip away the serrations along each side. Brush glue on the back of one leaf and stick in place in one of the quarter sections between the bands, pressing carefully around the curve. Attach the other three leaves in the same way.

5 From the pink paper, cut some strips measuring a scant ⅛ x 1½in (2mm x 4cm) and glue them to the blue leaves as veins. Make a couple of dots from the pink paper using the hole punch. Stick these in place at either end of the egg where the colored strips intersect.

paper corsage

You may never have thought of making a corsage from paper but there is no reason not to! The paper used here is fairly durable and is not likely to get much wear when worn as a corsage. You can be sure that it will be very much admired, especially as it is so colorful. The vivid blue paper is a soft, flexible wrapping paper with an embossed waffle texture, creating an interesting effect. Colored paper has been bonded to one side so that when the petals and stamens are rolled, it creates a two-tone effect. A brooch clasp is attached to the back of the corsage.

You will need

Small, sharp scissors
6in (15cm) squares of origami paper, in purple, red, mid-green, yellow, and light green
9 x 6¾in (23 x 17cm) piece of blue recycled paper with an embossed waffle texture
White (PVA) glue, wide brush, and small brush
Sharp pencil
Patterns for large petal, small petal, and leaf (see page 120)
Circle template ruler (optional)
Knitting needle
1½in (4cm) brooch clasp

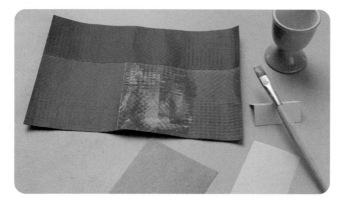

1 With scissors, cut the purple, red, mid-green, and yellow origami squares into smaller rectangles that will fit on the piece of blue waffle paper and will be large enough for you to cut out five large purple petals, five small red petals, two mid-green leaves, and three 1⅛in (3cm) yellow circles. Using the wide brush, spread the glue on one side of the waffle paper and stick the origami pieces in place.

2 With a pencil, draw around the large petal pattern to draw five large petals on the purple paper, and around the small petal pattern to draw five small petals on the red. Use a circle template ruler or the template on page 122 to draw three 1⅛in (3cm) circles on the yellow. Leave the mid-green area free for now. Cut out all the shapes with the scissors.

3 Referring to the patterns, cut slits down the center of each petal, starting at the base and leaving ⅜in (1cm) uncut at the top. With the small brush, apply glue to the red or purple side of a petal along one side of the split. Overlap the other side of the split onto the glue, and hold these edges together as the glue sets. Now curl each petal over a knitting needle, revealing the blue reverse side.

Tip: *Make a number of flowers and use them to decorate a hat. However, don't wear them in the rain, as they may degrade and the pigment in the paper may not be colorfast.*

4 Place a generous dab of glue on the base of one large petal and lay the bottom of a second large petal on this, so that this petal overlaps the first one slightly. Continue attaching the large outer petals in the same way, until the fifth petal overlaps the first. Now add the small red petals in the same manner until they complete the second layer of the flower.

5 Snip tiny segments all around the yellow circles—to make them evenly spaced, I find it easiest to snip segments opposite each other for the first eight snips and then to cut between these snips. Turn the circles over so that the blue side is on top, place your thumb in the center, and curl up the small cut sections against the side of your thumb.

6 Using the small brush, place a generous dab of glue in the center of the first circle, then add the second circle and press to stick firmly. Dab glue onto the center of this circle, and press the third circle into place on top. Curl the outside sections inward by pressing them together with your fingers.

7 Lay the leaf pattern on the light green origami paper, and draw around it twice to make two leaves. Cut the leaves out with the scissors. Referring to the pattern, cut a slit down the center starting at the base and leaving the top ⅝in (1.5cm) uncut. Cut a series of small snips along each side to create the leaf serrations. Apply glue to the backs of the leaves and stick onto the blue side of the mid-green/blue bonded paper. Cut around the leaves, leaving a blue margin at least ⅛in (3mm) all around.

8 Curl the tips of the leaves by wrapping them around the knitting needle. Stick them together at the base so that they slightly overlap each other. Leave them until the glue has dried.

9 Turn the flower over and stick the leaves firmly onto the back of the flower, making sure that the fronts of the leaves are facing forward. Apply a line of glue along the base, place the clasp along it, and secure by pasting at least three ⅜ x 1¼in (1 x 3cm) strips of blue paper over the clasp. Paint the outside of the strips with glue as an added protection.

paisley bookmark

The image of a plant growing in an urn is a favorite motif in the folk art tradition of papercutting. It is an ideal design for the classic technique of folding and cutting paper, most often without using a pattern, and then unfolding it to produce a symmetrical design. Even though it is a well-known technique, I think of it as magic. I have used a paisley wrapping paper for the main image, mounted on an unpatterned paper. This in turn is mounted on a slightly larger purple piece, which frames it. The flowers are made from circles of blue scrap paper and the urn has been distinguished by the addition of a few strips of the purple backing paper.

You will need

Cutting mat and metal ruler
Craft knife or scalpel
Lightweight cardstock in purple
Medium-weight paper in stone color
Brown paisley wrapping paper
Pattern for urn and plant (see page 119)
Sharp pencil
Small, sharp scissors
White (PVA) glue and brush
Scraps of lightweight construction (sugar) paper in blue
Circle template ruler

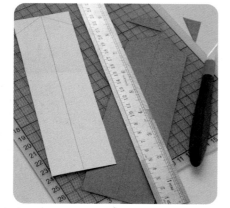

1 Using a cutting mat, a metal ruler, and a craft knife or scalpel, measure and cut out a 2 ³⁄₄ x 8in (7 x 20cm) rectangle from the purple cardstock and a 2 ¹⁄₄ x 7 ¹⁄₂in (6 x 19cm) rectangle from the stone-colored paper. On each rectangle, draw a line down the center lengthwise, and mark a point ³⁄₄ in (2cm) down from the top on each side. Place the ruler across the midpoint on the top edge and the marked point on one side; cut along this line with the craft knife. Repeat on the other side of the rectangle. Do the same for the second rectangle.

2 Cut out a 2 ¹⁄₄ x 7 ¹⁄₂in (6 x 19cm) rectangle from the patterned wrapping paper, and fold it in half lengthwise. Lay the straight side of the pattern along the fold. Draw carefully around the pattern with a pencil, then remove the pattern and cut out carefully with small, sharp scissors. The traditional way of cutting is to cut it out all at once, so that the discarded part is in one piece, but don't worry if you can't achieve this and have to cut it away in pieces.

3 Brush glue onto the back of the stone-colored piece. Stick it to the center of the purple cardstock piece so there is an even margin all around, smoothing it firmly. Cut a 2 x ³⁄₈in (5 x 1cm) strip of blue construction (sugar) paper by eye, so it looks uneven. Glue this centrally at the bottom edge of the stone-colored paper, to represent a plinth. Apply glue to the back of the urn and plant. Stick this shape centrally on the stone-colored background, so that the base of the urn sits on the plinth.

4 Fold a scrap of the blue paper in half and use the circle template ruler to draw five ³⁄₈in (1cm) circles on it. Cut them out and discard one, then brush glue onto the backs of the remaining nine circles. Stick one on the end of each branch. From the same paper, cut two ¹⁄₈in- (3mm-) wide strips slightly longer than the width of the urn at the top and at the base. Glue to the urn top and base. From the same paper, cut a long oval shape that will fit into the top of the urn, leaving a margin of brown showing around the edge; glue in place. Once dry, place the bookmark under a heavy book to flatten.

ANNUALS

[565]

Calendula—or pot Marigold—has vivid orange flowers and will thrive almost a...

oval box

A favorite color combination of mine is a mixture of purples and browns. One of the joys of working with colored paper is that you can use scraps to try out good color combinations. Your colors do not have to be literal, such as green for leaves and yellow for the centers of flowers. You can use whatever hues look right to you, and this freedom will help you to create more interesting designs. The colors on this pale mauve box lid are not at all naturalistic but are well suited to the simple shape. The design looks intricate but it is achieved by the layering of color and shapes for the flowers, contrasting with the simplicity of the leaves and branches. Before decorating it you could cover the box with your own paper (see Tip), or simply choose a box with a background color you like.

You will need

Patterns for flowers and leaves (see page 122)
Scraps of lightweight colored paper, such as origami paper
Sharp pencil
Small, sharp scissors
Pinking shears
Circle template ruler (optional)
White (PVA) glue and small brush
Dark brown lightweight paper
Cutting mat and craft knife or scalpel
8½ x 7in (22 x 18cm) oval papier-mâché box

1 Use the flower patterns to cut a selection of flower shapes from the colored papers, drawing around the patterns with a pencil and cutting out the shapes with small, sharp scissors. You will need a mixture of different sizes to build up the flowers.

2 Cut around the circumference of a couple of the larger circles using pinking shears to make a decorative edge. Snip small segments from the edge of the smaller circles. You will also need a few cut-out smaller circles in contrasting paper colors to finish the centers of some of the flowers, so use the circle template ruler to cut these out. (Or you could just take the sheet from which you have cut out the patterns for the flowers, lay the appropriate cut-out over the colored paper, draw a small circle inside it freehand, and then cut it out.)

3 You need to make five composite flowers by layering the different colors, shapes, and sizes, finishing each flower with either a small dot or a snipped circle. Build up the layers by carefully brushing a small amount of glue onto the back of each layer, pressing firmly so that the glue adheres evenly.

Tip: *Choose your paper colors to match your box color. It is easy to cover a box with lightweight, flexible paper before decorating it. Cut an oval the size of the lid top, plus an extra ⅝in (1.5cm) overlap all around. Cut a strip the size of the lid side, adding ⅝in (1.5cm) overlap to the lower edge. Cut another oval the size of the box base, with no overlap. Cut a strip the size of the box side, adding a ⅝in (1.5cm) overlap to both long edges. Snip into all the overlaps. Glue the lid oval to the top, gluing the overlap to the side of the lid, then glue the strip around the side, with its overlap inside the lid. Glue the box strip to the box side, with one overlap glued inside the box and the other glued to the base, then glue the oval to the base.*

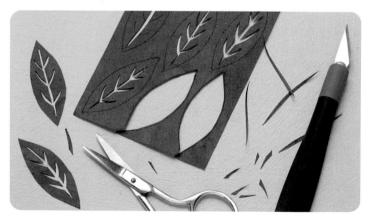

4 Use the leaf pattern and pencil to draw eight leaves on the dark brown paper. Also draw the veins on each of the leaves.

5 Cut out the leaves using a cutting mat and a craft knife or scalpel. Cut away narrow strips for the veins, which should reach a point toward the edge of the leaves. This needs to be done carefully but don't worry if you cut too far—it is easy to make another leaf!

6 Place the flowers around the edge of the top of the box lid but not at the base; do not glue them yet. Cut, freehand, some ¼in (5mm) strips from the brown paper, for a main stem and four smaller stems.

7 Roughly mark in pencil where the flowers will be, and then remove them temporarily. Lay the central stem and the four smaller stems in position. Cut the ends at an angle where these smaller side stems meet the central one. Brush glue onto the backs and press them in place.

8 Stick each flower in place at the end of each side branch. Press firmly to make sure that they stick properly.

9 Finally, brush glue sparingly onto the backs of the leaves (so that the glue won't ooze out of the leaf veins) and stick them in place. You need to stick two pairs along the main stem and one leaf on the lower edge of each side stem.

for the home
chapter 4

table mat

This is a quick and easy project to make. Only two colors have been used to make a strikingly stylized image of three flowers growing in a window box. You don't need an overcomplicated design—less is sometimes more! In fact, the repetition of one or two motifs to make an overall design is a well-known technique. The design is laminated with thick plastic so that it can serve as a wipe-clean table mat.

You will need

Large scissors
Two 10 x 8in (25 x 20cm) pieces of construction (sugar) paper, one in bright pink and one in lime green
9 ½ x 12in (24 x 30cm) piece of off-white watercolor paper
Sharp pencil
Small, sharp scissors
Patterns for leaf and window box (see page 125) and 1½in (4cm) circle (see page 122)
White (PVA) glue, small brush, and wide brush

1 Using large scissors, cut three ¼ x 9in (5mm x 23cm) strips from the pink paper. Lay them on the off-white watercolor paper, spacing them evenly.

Tip: *You could make a series of these pretty table mats incorporating names or initials of all the family into the design on the window box.*

2 Using a pencil and the circle pattern, draw three 1½in (4cm) circles on the pink paper. Cut them out with the small scissors. Snip eight small, equally spaced segments around the edge of each one to make a stylized flower. (To make them equidistant, snip segments opposite each other.) Lay them on top of the stems.

3 Using the leaf pattern, draw 36 leaves on the lime green paper. Cut out each one with the small scissors. Now cut a small slit partway down the center, as the central leaf vein. Place the leaves either side of the pink stems, adjusting the position of the stems to accommodate all the leaves without their touching each other. You will need six leaves on either side of each stem.

4 When you are happy with the position of all the elements, glue the bottom section of the stem in place, using the small brush to apply the glue. Draw a faint line where it will eventually be stuck down along the whole length. Stick each leaf in place so that the beginning of the leaves meets at this middle line. Finally, glue the pink stems over the edges of the leaves and stick the pink flowers in place at the top of the stems.

5 Cut a window box out of the pink paper using the pattern. From the lime green paper, cut a ¼ x 8in (5mm x 20.5cm) strip to fit on the top of the box and a ¼ x 7in (5mm x 17.5cm) strip to fit on the box ⅜in (1cm) from the bottom edge. You may have to trim these edges slightly so that they fit neatly. Glue them down and then, using the wide brush to apply the glue, stick the box centrally in place over the pink stems. Press to smooth.

In a house with young children you will often find a wall or door frame that is covered in pencil marks and dates. This growth chart can easily be attached to a wall and provides a decorative picture that young children will happily stand beside while you measure them.

wise owl growth chart

The wise owl and the pale, fluttering moth come out at night when young children are believed to grow. This measuring chart has marks for the measurements disguised as patterns on the bark all along the trunk of the tree. The chart is principally to show how much the child has grown, rather than how tall they are. Hang it in a bedroom and the friendly owl will be a kind and watchful presence over the sleeping child.

You will need

Patterns for tree, leaf, owl, owl
  breast, and moth (see page 122)
12 x 33in (30 x 84cm) piece of thick
  brown paper
Yellow waxy (chinagraph) pencil
  (or a colored or white pencil)
Large scissors
Small, sharp scissors
12 x 33in (30 x 84cm) piece and
  4 x 6in (10 x 15cm) piece of pale
  gray medium-weight paper
Sharp pencil and eraser
Long ruler (optional) and small ruler
6in (15cm) square of medium-weight
  brown paper
16in (40cm) square of lime green
  medium-weight paper
8 x 5in (18 x 13cm) piece of yellow
  construction (sugar) paper
Circle template ruler
White (PVA) glue, small brush, and
  wide brush
Spray adhesive
Hole punch

1 Lay the tree pattern on the thick brown paper rectangle so that the central trunk is off-center on the background. At the base there will be 6$\frac{1}{8}$in (15.5cm) to the left of the trunk and 3$\frac{3}{4}$in (9.5cm) to the right. Draw around the pattern using a yellow waxy (chinagraph) pencil. Cut along the lines with large scissors, and cut out the branches with small scissors. Remove the brown tree section marked by the pattern.

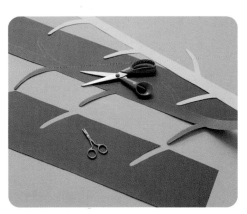

2 Lay both sides of the brown tree section on the large rectangle of pale gray paper, making sure that the straight sides, top, and base match the corresponding edges. With a pencil, draw inside the lines of the tree onto the gray background, transferring the tree outline.

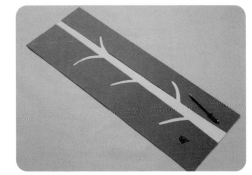

3 Remove the brown paper and draw a straight line down the center of the tree trunk, using a pencil and a long ruler or the straight edge of one of the pieces of brown paper. Now use a small ruler to mark each $\frac{1}{2}$in (1cm) all the way to the top of the tree.

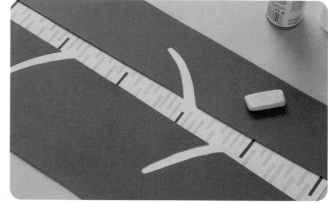

4 By hand, cut some ¼in (4mm) x 1½in–2in (4–5cm) strips from the lime green paper—you'll need 55 if your marks are every ½in (or 72 if they are every 1cm). Cut some strips the same size from the medium-weight brown paper—six if your marks are every ½in (nine if every 1cm). Stick a brown strip across the trunk at the first ½in (1cm) mark—it should reach just across the middle. Continue sticking green strips across the trunk at each mark, reaching various distances across the trunk but never completely crossing it, to look like bark. Add a brown strip after every eleven green ½in-marks (nine 1cm-marks).

5 First rub away any remaining pencil lines using a clean eraser, being sure to brush away the debris. Working outdoors or in a well-ventilated space, spray the adhesive onto the back of the brown paper to the right of the tree (after checking its position). Allow the glue to become sticky, then press the piece into place to the right of the tree, matching up the outside edges. Repeat with the other side of the tree.

6 With the pencil, draw around the leaf pattern on the lime green paper—you'll need 12 leaves. Cut out the leaves with the small scissors. Cut a thin long segment out of the middle of each leaf and arrange the leaves on the ends of the branches, with three each for the two lower branches on the left and two each for the remaining three branches. Glue in place.

7 Use the patterns to cut out the owl body from the yellow paper and the owl breast from the brown paper. Use the circle template ruler to cut two 1¼in (3cm) circles for the eyes from the gray paper. Cut two ⅜in (1cm) circles from the brown paper to use as the center of the eyes. Stick the breast into position on the lower section of the owl's body. Stick the two eyes in place, adding the brown circles in the centers. Cut a small triangle from the brown paper for the beak and stick it below the eyes. Cut two identical eyebrows from a folded piece of the brown paper. Stick them in place over the eyes.

Tip: *To make the chart more durable it would be a good idea to laminate it. To make it easy to hang on the wall, add two eyelets at the top, through which to thread a cord.*

8 Apply glue to the back of the owl using the wider glue brush and press into place so that the claws sit just over the top left-hand branch. Smooth over with your hands. Draw around the moth pattern on a small piece of the gray paper and cut out. Stick the moth midway between the two branches on the right side of the tree. Add two ⅛in (3mm) yellow circles for eyes on the head of the moth. Add a small brown dot in the center of each eye, cutting these out with the small hole punch.

blossom *frame*

This charming project combines the complementary arts of papercutting and paper sculpture. The background is made from a fine corrugated cardboard in a pale lilac color, stuck to foam board and then cut into a circular shape that would make a lovely mirror frame. The beautiful white paper flowers look difficult to make but are surprisingly easy to create—you only need patience and deft fingers, and you will be well rewarded if you carefully follow the directions. You could also surround the frame with flowers and leaves using the same techniques.

You will need

12in (30cm) square of foam board
Cutting mat
Dinner plate about 10½in (27cm) in diameter
Sharp pencil
Craft knife or scalpel
Saucer about 5½in (14cm) in diameter
18in (45cm) square of fine corrugated cardboard, in lilac
White (PVA) glue and brush
Patterns for three sizes of petals, stem, and leaf (see page 121)
White medium-weight cartridge paper
Small, sharp scissors
Knitting needle
Dry ballpoint pen

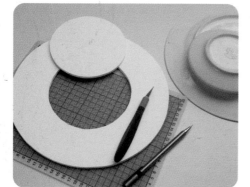

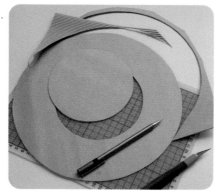

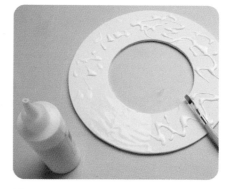

1 Place the foam board on the cutting mat, and place the dinner plate on top. Draw around the plate with a pencil, then cut out the circle with a craft knife or scalpel. Put the saucer in the center of this circle and draw around it. Cut out the circle with the craft knife or scalpel.

2 Place the corrugated cardboard on the cutting mat with the smooth side on top, and draw around the two plates as you did in step 1.

3 Squeeze the glue onto the foam board and smooth out with a brush.

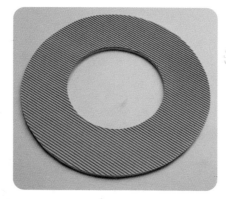

4 Lay the corrugated board, right side up, on top of the foam board. Press lightly but firmly so that the glue adheres evenly. You could turn the circle over and lay a couple of books on top to help the glue to stick.

Tip: *Although there is something refined about white flowers, you may like to introduce some color. Remember that you'll need to use a similar medium-weight cartridge paper.*

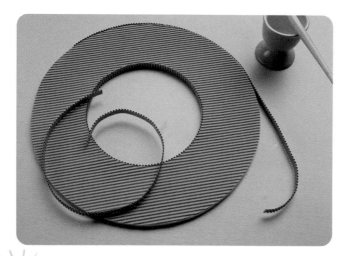

5 From the corrugated cardboard, cut three ⅜ x 18in (8mm x 45cm) strips, all with the ridges going across the width, not along the length. Apply glue to the outer edge of the frame and press two strips in place to cover the glued outer edge, cutting off the excess at the ends. Press firmly to make sure the glue sticks well. Glue the third strip to the inner edge in the same way.

6 Place the patterns on the cartridge paper, draw around them, and with the scissors cut out four large petals, five medium petals, and twelve small petals.

7 Cut a slit ⅝in (1.5cm) long at the middle of the base on each of the large and medium petals, and a slightly shorter slit on each of the smaller petals. To create the three-dimensional effect, brush some glue onto the back of a petal alongside the slit and stick one side over the other, holding until the glue is set. Repeat for the other petals. Curl the top edges of the petals by gently curling them around a knitting needle.

8 Stick the petals together to make the flowers, gluing and overlapping the base of each petal. Use the four large petals for the large flower, the five medium petals for the medium flower, and four small petals each for the three small flowers.

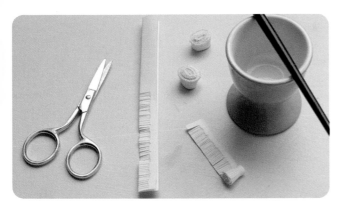

9 For the flower stamens, cut a 2 x 5in (5 x 13cm) strip of the cartridge paper and fold it in half lengthwise. Make close-together snips along the folded side that go two-thirds of the way across. Open out, and cut along the fold line. You now have two strips, one for the large flower and one for the medium flower. Put some glue along the uncut long edge of each strip and roll up tightly. Cut three 2 x 2½ in (5 x 6.5cm) strips and make these into smaller rolls for the three small flowers.

10 Stick one large stamen into the large flower and one into the medium flower using a good dab of glue on each. Glue a small stamen into each of the three small flowers. When the glue is dry, use a knitting needle to open out the stamens.

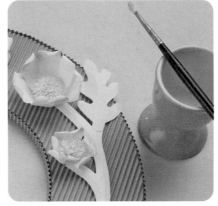

11 Lay the patterns for the stem and the leaf on a small piece of the cartridge paper and draw around it. Turn each pattern over and draw around it again to get a reversed image, to use on the opposite side of the frame. With the dry ballpoint pen, score along the center of the stems and mark the fold lines for the leaves. Cut out the stems and leaves with the scissors.

12 With the stems and leaves right side up, bend them away from you along the scored lines. Experiment with their positions on the frame, and then add a few points of glue on the back where each stem touches the frame, and stick in place. Glue the leaves to the frame in a similar way.

13 Stick the flowers in place at the ends of the branches, putting a large dab of glue under each flower and leaving until the glue is thoroughly set.

tree of life picture

The tree of life is a beautiful symbolic motif signifying growth, development, and new life, and one that lends itself well to the craft of papercutting. Traditional papercutting techniques have exploited the use of symmetry, and folding a piece of paper before cutting a design is a simple way to achieve this. Even though you can predict the outcome of your cut design, when you unfold the paper the result is always surprising. In this project, as a variation on the traditional motif, I used old stamps for the flower centers. The miniature designs are lovely and work well when incorporated into a papercut design. Stamps are easy to find—you may even have a collection from your childhood stored away in an album.

You will need

Cutting mat and metal ruler
Craft knife or scalpel
Fairly stiff Mi-Teintes pastel paper, in
    brown and lime green
Patterns for tree, flower, and urn
    (see page 122)
Masking tape
Sharp pencil
Construction (sugar) paper, in buff,
    light pink, and dark pink
White (PVA) glue and small brush
Small, sharp scissors
Assorted postage stamps

1 Using the cutting mat, metal ruler, and craft knife or scalpel, cut a 10 x 8½in (25 x 22cm) piece of the brown paper. Fold it in half lengthwise and place the tree pattern on top of the folded paper, with the straight side of the pattern along the fold. Secure it in a few places with some narrow strips of masking tape. With the pencil, draw carefully around the pattern.

2 Still using the cutting mat, cut away the areas between the drawn lines with the craft knife, removing the cut pieces as you go. Take great care not to cut through the branches, and pay particular attention to the points where leaf and branch meet as these are areas that may tear away if the paper is not cleanly cut through.

Tip: *If you want to frame the image, you could mount the green paper onto a thicker, ivory mount prior to framing.*

3 Unfold the tree and mark the central vein of each leaf with a pencil. Cut the buff-colored paper into 1¼ x ⅜in (3 x 1cm) strips. Lay one of these strips against the pencil line on a leaf, and carefully cut away the small section that overlaps the stem. Repeat for some of the other leaves. Brush the glue sparingly onto the back of these strips and stick each on its leaf.

Here the papercut picture is pinned to a door, but if you wish to preserve it, it is best to protect it under glass in a simple frame.

4 Turn over the tree and carefully cut away the buff paper extending beyond the edge of each leaf. Now turn the tree over again and repeat the process for a few more leaves, trimming off the excess of these and gluing them in place before adding more strips. Continue in this way till all the leaves are covered. This makes it easier to work with.

5 Using the pencil and the flower pattern, draw four flowers each on the light pink and dark pink papers. Now draw four equidistant intersecting lines to make an eight-pointed star. Cut out the circles with scissors.

6 With the scissors, snip small segments out of the circles using the pencil lines as guides, to make the radiating petals. You can make two snips for each guideline, but not more.

7 Cut circles out of the stamps—the size of a circle will depend on the size of the stamp. Snip segments out of the stamps to make petals (it isn't necessary to draw guidelines first).

8 Cut a piece of the lime-green paper 11in (28cm) wide and 12in (30 cm) deep. Use the urn pattern to mark where the bottom of the tree should be—the top of the urn will be where the lower branches begin, and the bottom of the urn even with the bottom of the card. Apply glue sparingly to the back of the tree and press into place centrally on the green paper. Place a heavy book over the tree to help the glue adhere evenly.

9 Paint glue carefully onto the backs of the flowers and stick one in place at the end of each branch, alternating the colors. Be careful not to use too much glue on the petals as you do not want any glue stains to show up on the front of your picture. Press the flowers down well so that the glue adheres evenly.

10 Glue a stamp circle in the center of each flower, balancing the colors of the stamps evenly around the design.

11 Stick some stamp circles directly onto the trunk and along the branches, positioning them symmetrically over the tree.

12 Cut a 4in (10cm) square of the brown paper and a 4 x 2in (10 x 5cm) rectangle from each of the light pink and dark pink papers. Glue these two pink rectangles onto the brown square so that they meet at the center and the edges are even with those of the brown square. Press flat to make sure the glue adheres. Lay the urn pattern in the center of this two-tone square and draw around it with the pencil.

13 Cut out the urn and stick it in place at the bottom of the picture so it is centered on the trunk and the lower edge is even with the bottom of the card. Press firmly as the glue sets. Leave overnight under a heavy book so that the picture stays flat.

leaf place cards

The leaf decoration on these elegant place cards looks as if it has been carved from wood coated in gold leaf. In fact, they are very simply made from gold coated paper. The intriguing three-dimensional effect is created by scoring and gently folding the paper, while the border along the base is made from the same paper folded over and snipped along the fold. This is a technique that can be applied to a number of papercutting projects. The leaves have been mounted on ivory-white watercolor paper—this has a lovely surface texture that adds to the stylish finish.

You will need

Stiff ivory-white watercolor paper
Cutting mat and metal ruler
Craft knife or scalpel
Sharp pencil
Bone scorer (a dull-edged tool used for making sharp fold lines)
Patterns for two leaves (see page 124)
Gold coated art paper (a recycled, textured paper)
Metal knitting needle
Small, sharp scissors
White (PVA) glue and brush

1 For each place card, use a cutting mat, metal ruler, and craft knife or scalpel to cut the watercolor paper to measure 6¾ x 4¾in (17 x12cm). Measure and mark halfway along both long sides with a pencil, line up the ruler with these points, and score a line between them with a bone scorer. Bend the paper with the scored line on the inside.

2 Draw around the patterns onto the back of the gold paper, using a sharp pencil, taking special care around the leaf serrations.

Tip: *As well as folding the gold paper for a three-dimensional effect, be careful to press the glued edges of the leaves onto the background without flattening them.*

3 Place the gold paper on a yielding surface, such as a sheet of construction (sugar) paper folded into quarters. Draw the leaf veins on the backs of the leaves as guidelines for scoring. These lines should meet the points around the edge of the chestnut leaf, and should end in the middle of the lobes of the oak leaf. Use the pointed end of the knitting needle to score along the penciled lines.

These sumptuous card placements will add a real touch of class to your tea or dinner table. You could write the initials of your guests above the leaves or, if you prefer not to mark the front of the card, write the complete name inside.

 **4** Using small, sharp scissors, cut out the leaves, paying particular attention to the outer curves and serrations.

5 Turn the leaves so that the gold side is facing upward, and bend or fold them along the lines that have been scored on the back. For added effect you could also make a gentle fold between the scored lines.

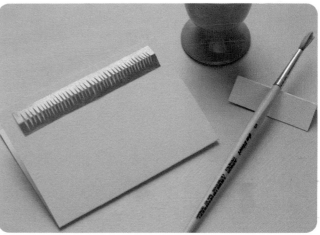

6 Cut a 4 x ¾ in (10 x 2cm) strip of gold paper, and fold it in half lengthwise. Using the scissors, snip little segments into the folded edge all along the length. Snip through both layers but make sure you don't cut all the way through to the other edge.

7 Open up this strip and experiment with its positioning before actually gluing it in place. For the center of the strip to stand up a little, creating the three-dimensional effect, the long edges are pushed inward slightly and only these edges are stuck in place. Brush small amounts of glue onto the back along the long edges, and glue the strip along the bottom of the place card, pushing the edges inward a little and sticking it in place without pressing the paper flat.

8 Brush small amounts of glue onto only a few points/lobes on the back of the leaf—do not apply any glue to the middle of the leaf. Press onto the card, creating the same three-dimensional effect as in step 7. Finally, add each guest's initials to the card above the leaves.

seed packets

Like many gardeners, I like to save my own seeds and share them with friends and fellow enthusiasts. I use boring brown envelopes for myself, but if I want to give some treasured seeds to a friend, I like to make a simple decorated package. The little envelopes are made from construction (sugar) paper, and the colorful motifs decorating them are cut from seed catalogs. These typically have very intense colors, no doubt to get you into gardening mode when you are reading the catalogs in the depths of winter! If you are saving vegetable seed, you could cut up images of the appropriate vegetables for the motifs decorating the envelopes. The instructions are for one seed packet.

You will need

Sharp pencil
Patterns for seed packet and plant in pot (see page 119)
Construction (sugar) paper in yellow-green and light brown
Small, sharp scissors
Metal ruler
Bone scorer (a dull-edged tool used for making sharp fold lines)
White (PVA) glue and brush
Assorted seed catalog images
Circle template ruler

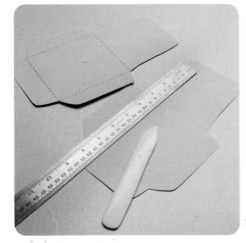

1 With the pencil, draw around the seed packet pattern on the paper, and cut out the shape carefully using the scissors. Line up the metal ruler over each of the dotted fold lines and use the bone scorer to score the lines.

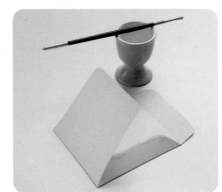

2 Bend the packet along the folds, and apply glue to the edges that are to be stuck down, leaving the top edge unglued. Press the glued edges together.

3 Choose a colorful section from a seed catalog image and fold it in half. Lay the plant pattern on it with the straight side of the pattern along the fold in the paper. Draw around the pattern, remove it, and cut out the shape with the scissors. Open out the shape.

4 Use the circle template ruler to draw a 1⅛in (3cm) circle on a flower from the seed catalog images. Remove the pattern and cut out the circle. Snip out small segments all around the circumference. Glue the plant from step 3 and this flower in place on the left side of the packet front.

Gather seeds on a dry day, seal the envelopes, and store in a cool, dry place. Don't forget to write the names of the seeds on the packets.

jam labels

I often think I'd like to make some jam labels to identify my homemade jam, but I always seem to have made the jam before I think of the labels! This project shows you how to design and make one-off labels that will certainly shout out from the pantry shelves. For jars of preserves given as presents, these graphic, colorful labels are ideal, and you hardly need to wrap them further if you cover them in similar paper. As an alternative to one-off labels, you could design your own and either color-photocopy them or scan them and run them off on a home printer. If you do that, remember to leave space for the name of the contents and the date.

You will need

Pattern for apple (see page 125)
Lightweight, flexible paper such as origami paper, in white, red, and pink
Sharp pencil
Cutting mat and craft knife or scalpel
Small, sharp scissors
Bookbinder's paste (50 percent PVA) and brush

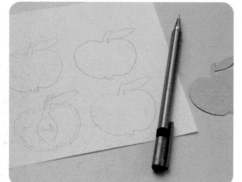

1 Lay the apple pattern on a square of white origami paper and draw around it with the sharp pencil, once for each label. Remove the pattern and draw the internal markings (the seeds, core, and around the inner edge of the apple) freehand.

2 Using a cutting mat, cut away the fine internal lines with a craft knife or scalpel. This is quite delicate work, and if you don't want to make these cuts you can simply omit them. Using the scissors or the craft knife or scalpel, cut out the apples, and snip out small sections along each side of the leaves.

3 Cut out a 2¼ x 4in (6 x 10cm) rectangle from the red paper and a 1¼ x 2¼in (3 x 6cm) strip from the pink paper for each label. Apply paste to the back of the pink strip and stick in place on top of the red rectangle, aligning the bottom edges and leaving a small strip of red showing on the right. Smooth out to remove any wrinkles or bubbles.

4 For each label, carefully brush the paste onto the back of the apple and then stick in place on the red and pink background, positioning the apple so that the pink paper appears behind one seed and the red behind the other.

These vibrant pink and red jam labels are complemented by tying a circle of the same paper around the lid.

shelf edging

For some reason I love old letters—perhaps it is partly because they are becoming so rare these days. Now that friends know that I am a hoarder of such things, they occasionally hand me a little package of family letters that are no longer wanted but cannot be casually thrown away. The handwriting styles and the color of the various writing papers make them well suited to use as a subtle decoration, such as this simple shelf edging. Of course, the content of the letters is an added interest. In fact, reusing old letters and other papers is a common practice all over the world.

You will need

Spray adhesive (or bookbinder's paste if you prefer, but you'd need to iron the letters flat when the glue is dry)
Selection of old letters— as the average size of a letter is 8¼ x 6in (21 x 15cm), I used seven to make two 3 ½ x 35½in (9 x 90cm) strips
8 x 39in (20 x 100cm) piece of laid paper (which has a finely ribbed appearance) in cream, cut from a large sheet
Sharp pencil and ruler
Large scissors
Pattern for triangle (see page 121)
Small, sharp scissors
Large hole punch
Scrap of cardstock

1 Working outdoors or in a well-ventilated space, spray the back of each letter with the adhesive and stick in place across the backing paper, butting up the edges and aligning them with the long bottom edge of the backing paper. Smooth over with your hands. Draw a straight line through the letters 3½in (9cm) from the long bottom edge of the backing. With large scissors, cut along this line to make a strip measuring 3½ x 35½in (9 x 90cm)—if you have more letters, you may use the whole 39in (100cm) but this may mean losing part of a letter. Trim the remaining strip to the same width.

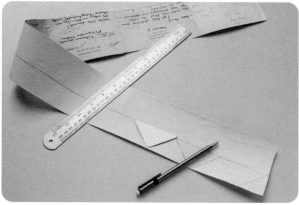

2 Turn the strip over so that the cream paper is on top. Draw a line along the length of the strip 1½in (4cm) from the bottom long edge. Starting at one end, place the triangle pattern with the rounded point downward, and the long, straight side against the line. Draw around the pattern, then move it along the line so that it is adjacent to the previous shape, and repeat. Continue in this way until you reach the end of the strip.

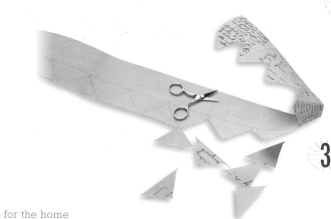

3 Use small, sharp scissors to cut away the triangles, taking particular care with the rounded points at the bottom.

4 With the hole punch, make a hole in the center of each triangle ⅝in (1.5cm) from the rounded point. To make neat holes, place a small piece of cardstock behind the paper, and punch through both layers. The resistance to the sharp edge of the punch made by cutting through a thicker layer means that the hole is punched with a neater edge.

Tip: *You can attach the shelf edging by folding over ¾in (2cm) on the straight side of the strip and attaching this edge to the shelf with double-sided tape or flat-headed pins. An alternative would be to line the shelf with paper up to the edge of the shelf and stick the edging to the paper lining.*

child's wall frieze

This charming frieze has been inspired by that enduring children's toy, the paper doll, which traditionally comes with clothes attached by bending the paper tabs on the clothes over to the back of the cut-out doll. I loved paper dolls as a child, and now I am making the very same toys for my granddaughters. The dolls in this project have already been dressed but you could make them with children, who love cutting and sticking. This is a perfect project for using up scraps of paper, as you do not need large pieces. The dresses here have been made from handmade wrapping paper but any patterned paper will do.

You will need

Patterns for doll, dress, apron, blouse, and hair (see page 123)
Lightweight paper in pale pink
Sharp pencil
Small, sharp scissors
Cutting mat
Craft knife or scalpel
6¼ x 4¾ in (16 x 12cm) piece of patterned wrapping paper for each dress
6in (15cm) squares of origami paper in bright pink, red, and orange
Scraps of origami paper in brown, green, and yellow, or colors of your choice
White (PVA) glue, wide brush, and small brush
Pinking shears
18 x 12in (46 x 30cm) piece of yellow-green construction (sugar) paper
Circle template ruler
Spray adhesive
26 x 12in (66 x 31cm) piece of pink mounting board

1 Place the doll pattern on a 6 x 12in (15 x 30cm) piece of the pale pink paper. With a pencil, draw around the outline of the shape, and then cut it out with small, sharp scissors. Now place the doll on a cutting mat and use the craft knife or scalpel to cut out the areas under the bent arms. (You could cut all three dolls from a piece of paper of this size. If you wish, fold it into thirds first, to allow you to cut them out all at one time.)

2 To cut out a dress, lay the dress pattern on the patterned wrapping paper, draw around it, and cut it out. Do the same with the other patterns and the origami paper, cutting out a bright pink apron, a red blouse, and finally some brown hair.

3 Brush glue onto the back of the blouse and stick in place on the doll's body. Repeat to glue the hair to the head. Add the dress on top of the blouse, followed by the pink apron. Any pale pink that is revealed around the edges can be cut away with the scissors. Press firmly to make sure that the surface is smooth and all the layers are well stuck down.

4 On a piece of the red paper, use the small scissors to cut a gentle curve that matches the curve on the bottom edge of the dress. Draw the same curve ⅜in (8mm) below the first one, and cut along that line with pinking shears. Cut three ⅛ x 3in (4mm x 8cm) strips with the scissors, making them slightly uneven to emphasize that they have been hand cut. Glue these three strips in place on the apron so that they appear to be radiating out from the waist.

5 Glue the curved red strip onto the hem of the skirt so that the pinked edge overlaps the lower edge of the skirt. Cut a ⅜ x 1⅜in (1 x 3.5cm) strip of orange paper for the waistband (checking the length on the doll before cutting). Glue it in place. Cut out and stick small rectangles of red paper on the feet so that they cover the shoes—they will probably be about 1¼ x ⅝in (3 x 1.5cm)—making sure that the tops don't reach above the ankles.

6 Turn over the doll and cut away the excess paper that sticks out around each foot.

7 Cut a 9 x 5in (23 x 13cm) rectangle of the yellow-green construction (sugar) paper, emphasizing its uneven, hand-cut quality. Now cut an uneven 3 x ¾in (8 x 2cm) rectangle of green paper and glue it in place ⅜in (1cm) from the bottom edge of the yellow-green paper and equidistant from the sides. With the larger brush, apply glue to the back of the doll and stick in place so she stands on the green strip. Using a circle template ruler, cut out two ⅛in (3mm) green circles for the eyes, and stick on the face. Cut a small, smiling red mouth and glue it under the eyes.

8 Make two more dolls, varying the colors and patterns of the clothes, and mount them onto the yellow-green paper as before. Working outdoors or in a well-ventilated space, spray the adhesive onto the backs of all three rectangles. Following the instructions carefully and allowing the glue to become sticky, space them evenly on the pink mounting board, with an even margin all around and between the dolls.

Tip: *Save used wrapping paper throughout the year—you will be sure to find some pretty scraps to use as dresses on the dolls. Always iron any scraps of used paper to make them flat and crinkle-free.*

butterflies *on wire*

These delicate butterflies appear to be floating in space but are actually attached to fine florist's wire, which is strong enough to hold them up without being noticeable. It is also flexible enough that they could be attached to a branch to make a summer room decoration. Or you may prefer just to display them in a vase. The peacock-blue paper used for the undersides of the butterflies' wings contrasts beautifully with the tops, made from vintage sheet music, which resembles the natural patterning found on butterflies' wings. Cutting through a simple design creates wonderful shadows when the butterflies are held behind a light source.

You will need

Ruler and sharp pencil
Scrap paper for pattern for butterfly body
Cutting mat
Craft knife or scalpel
6in (15cm) square of blue construction (sugar) paper
White (PVA) glue and brush
Two knitting needles, one fine and one thick
Covered (white) florist's wire, medium-thick and 8in (20cm) long
Butterfly pattern (see page 126)
Scraps of old sheet music
Small, sharp scissors
Sheet of peacock-blue origami paper
Bone scorer (a dull-edged tool used for making sharp fold lines)
Hole punch

1 With a ruler and pencil, draw on scrap paper a shape similar to a long triangle, 5½in (14cm) long, 1½in (4cm) wide at one end, and ¼in (5mm) wide at the other end. (For how to draw this, see Tip.) Place on a cutting mat and cut out with a craft knife or scalpel. Draw around this pattern on the construction (sugar) paper and cut out one of these shapes for each butterfly. You could cut two at once by folding the construction paper in half first. Brush glue onto the back of the shape, lay the fine knitting needle on the pasted side along the wider end, and begin to roll the paper tightly around the needle.

2 Continue rolling the paper around the needle until you are 1½in (4cm) from the narrow end. Bend ¾in (2cm) over at one end of the florist's wire and lay the wire across the paper, with the bent end parallel to the roll and the rest of the needle at right angles to the roll. Add a dab of glue and roll up tightly, enclosing the wire. Pull out the needle and repeat for the other butterflies.

Tip: *To draw the shape for step 1, draw a line to the desired length of the shape, with two shorter lines at the ends, at right angles to it and with half of each line on either side. Now connect up the ends of the two shorter lines.*

3 Place the butterfly pattern on the sheet music, draw around it once for each butterfly, and cut out the shapes neatly with scissors. Glue the sheet-music butterfly shapes to the blue origami paper, pressing firmly; allow to dry. Cut around the butterfly shapes so that you end up with butterfly shapes that each have a patterned top and a blue underside.

4 Lay the ruler along each join between the wings and the body on the blue underside of each butterfly, and score a fold line with the bone scorer. With the hole punch, make holes in the wings—two on each larger wing and one on each smaller wing. Using the craft knife and the cutting mat, cut two slits on each wing radiating out from the body.

5 With the blue underside facing, fold the wings away from you along the scored lines, refolding from the other side if necessary. Place the thicker knitting needle so it runs down the middle of the blue underside, then curl the butterfly shape around it to create a hollow along the butterfly body. Dab on some glue and lay the rolled paper body in this hollow, with the wire coming out of the bottom (near the smaller wings). Prop the wire up against something until the glue has set.

6 For the antennae, use scissors to cut a 3in (8cm) length of florist's wire for each butterfly; bend it in half. Use the knitting needle to push some glue into the hole at the head end of the butterfly (near the larger wings). Push the doubled end of the wire into the hole, and then add another blob of glue. Allow the glue to dry before turning the butterflies right side up.

alphabet *blocks*

Inspired by the wonderful 19th-century tradition of decorating wooden blocks with printed-paper images, these pretty blocks have been decorated with colored papers and vintage wallpaper scraps. The graphic images of friendly creatures are simple to make—I think they already have their own personalities! The instructions are for one owl block, but the animals are so simple that the instructions and pattern can easily be adapted for a cat or a panda block, or another of your choice. If you wish, the blocks could be decorated so they are like cube jigsaws—carefully choosing six different pictures for each of six blocks, and using them in the same order on the blocks, will create a set of blocks that form coherent images when correctly arranged together.

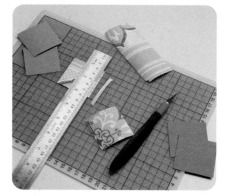

1 Use the cutting mat, ruler, and craft knife or scalpel to cut out three pairs of 2in (5cm) paper squares—two from vintage or retro wallpaper, two from one solid color (such as brown), and two from another solid color (such as gray)—for each block. You can use the grid on the cutting mat to cut the squares to the right size. (It is safer to cut the paper squares very slightly larger than the finished size, as the excess can be removed later, whereas you cannot add any if you cut them too small.)

2 Brush glue onto the surface of the wood block rather than onto the paper, and then stick each pair of matching papers onto opposite sides of the cube. Press the paper down firmly so that it lies flat on the surface.

3 Lay the owl pattern on a small piece of brown origami paper, draw around the shape with a pencil, and cut out with scissors. Brush glue evenly onto the back and stick it in place on one of the gray sides of the block.

4 Using a circle template ruler, draw two ⅜in (1cm) circles on a light-colored paper, cut out, and glue them on the owl's face as eyes. Cut a tiny triangle for the beak from the same paper, and glue this just below the eyes. Use the hole punch to cut two smaller circles from the gray paper and glue one to each eye, slightly below center.

5 Cut a semicircular piece from the retro wallpaper, choosing a portion with a small-scale pattern, and glue in place below the beak, with the straight edge even with the bottom edge of the block.

6 Select a letter on the alphabet-print paper, and cut around it with scissors. Glue in place on the brown side of the block adjacent to the image of the owl. When dry, apply two coats of varnish, allowing it to dry between coats.

papercut peacock

This colorful bird has been directly inspired by Polish peasant papercuts. I have a large collection of these and they are truly beautiful—so vibrant and immediate. It is unlikely that a pattern was ever used for this skilled and direct form of papercutting. I think it is worth aiming to be so accomplished that you can use your scissors to cut rather as you would use a pen to draw a confident and graceful line. Historic folk art draws on images that describe the small world of the rural village, so it is not surprising that creatures, flowers, and scenes from village life are the most common motifs. Birds are wonderful to illustrate, as you don't need to be realistic and can use as many bright colors as you like.

You will need

Patterns for peacock, wings, and tail feathers (see page 126)
12in (30cm) square of medium-weight paper in duck-egg blue
Sharp pencil
Small, sharp scissors
Pieces of origami paper at least 4in (10cm) square, in dark blue, peacock blue, bright pink, orange, yellow, and red
White (PVA) glue and brush
Two hole punches, one small and one large
Scrap of pale pink origami paper (for eye)
Small piece of lightweight paper in mid-brown
Spray adhesive
13in (33cm) square of white medium-weight cartridge paper
Sheet of scrap paper

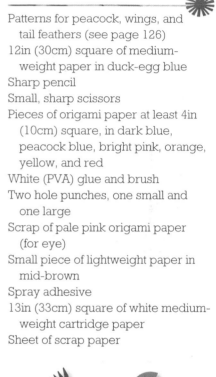

1 Lay the pattern for the peacock on the duck-egg blue paper. Draw around it with a pencil and cut it out with scissors.

2 Use the three wing patterns and eight tail-feather patterns to cut out the following pieces from origami paper: wing feathers (large dark blue, medium-size peacock blue, small bright pink), upper tail feathers (large orange, medium-size yellow, small red), middle tail feathers (large peacock blue, small red), and lower tail feathers (large red, medium-size bright pink, small dark blue). Keep them in their groups after cutting them out.

3 Cut small snips into the ends of the colored wing and tail pieces to create a feathery, hand-cut effect. You can vary these by making some snips larger and some smaller. For example, the orange piece for the upper tail section has only two wide segments cut out. Continue to keep the pieces in groups.

4 Brush glue on the back of the wing-feather pieces, and then stick the dark blue piece in the center of the peacock's breast. Stick the peacock-blue piece on top of it, and then the bright pink piece on top of that.

5 Glue the tail-feather pieces onto the tail in the same way, sticking down the largest piece in each group first, then adding the medium-size piece (there isn't one on the middle section), and finishing with the smallest piece on top. For the eye, use the hole punches to make a larger pale pink circle and a smaller brown circle. Glue the pink circle on the head, and the brown circle on top of the pink one.

6 Draw and cut out an orange feather and a pale pink feather, each about ⅜ x 1in (1 x 2.5cm), and cut several snips in the end of each. Glue them, overlapping, about ⅜in (1cm) below the eye. Cut a 1 x 7in (2.5 x 17.5cm) strip from brown paper. Fold it in half lengthwise, and cut small snips all along the fold—snip through both layers but cut only about two-thirds of the way to the other edge. Open it out.

7 Working outdoors or in a well-ventilated space, spray adhesive onto the back of the brown strip and peacock. Glue the strip 1½in (4cm) from the base of the white square, equidistant from the sides. Stick the peacock in place equidistant from the sides, with the feet on the brown strip. Lay scrap paper over it and smooth over firmly with your hands so that the adhesive adheres well.

paper *chandelier*

This festive little paper chandelier is made from two flat parts slotted together to make a three-dimensional shape. I used a double-sided cardstock, which is a different color on each side. One is pink/blue, and the other orange/gray, which means that one side of the chandelier shows pink and orange, and the other side gray and blue. To complete the decoration, I made tiny paper tassels and threaded them through holes in the branches of the chandelier. Origami paper is best for this as it is very thin and winds up into a small roll.

You will need

Pattern for chandelier (see page 126)
Two 12in (30cm) pieces of light- to medium-weight double-sided cardstock, one in pink/blue, the other in orange/gray
Sharp pencil
Cutting mat and metal ruler
Craft knife or scalpel
White (PVA) glue and brush
Hole punch
Scraps of origami paper in pink, red, orange, and purple
Small, sharp scissors
Fine hemp string in purple
Fine knitting needle

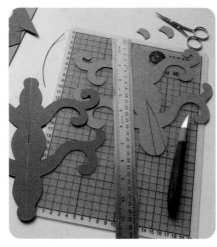

1 Place the pattern on the pink/blue piece of cardstock and draw around it with a pencil. Using a cutting mat and craft knife or scalpel, cut out the shape. Repeat for the orange/gray piece of cardstock.

2 On the orange/gray shape, cut away the top and bottom bulges, following the curve of the bulges beneath/above them. Draw a line down the center of each of the two shapes, and mark the center point. On the orange/gray piece, use the craft knife, ruler, and cutting mat to cut a slit exactly as thick as your cardstock, along the top half of the line—in other words, along the line from the center mark to the edge. On the pink/blue piece, cut a slit of exactly the same width along the bottom half of the line.

3 Slide the two parts together, pushing the slit in the orange/gray piece up through the slit in the pink/blue piece. Check they are pushed in fully. At the top of the pink/blue piece, cut a thin vertical slit ¼ in (5mm) long in the center of the second bulge (the one beneath the outer, small bulge). Cut a ¼ x ¾ in (5mm x 2cm) strip from orange/gray cardstock, and insert into the small slit in the pink/blue piece, with the gray side outward. Brush some glue onto the (orange) back of this strip. Press it against the adjacent (gray) side of the chandelier piece. Hold until the glue sticks. This will keep the chandelier's branches at right angles to each other.

Use this chandelier as a seasonal decoration. It looks pretty hung in a window, but would look particularly festive suspended over a Christmas table.

4 From a scrap of blue cardstock, cut a small piece and glue it over the split base of the pink/blue section, sticking it on the blue side. Use the hole punch to make holes in the top and bottom of the chandelier (in the center of the outer, small bulge at top and bottom). Also make three holes in each of the four branches: one at the end of the bottom curl on both the upper and lower branches, and one at the center of the lower branch.

5 Cut one 1 x 6in (2.5 x 15cm) strip of each of the pink, red, and orange origami papers. Glue the three strips together along the top edge, using just a small amount of glue. With scissors, along one long side make close-together snips that go two-thirds of the way across the width through all three layers. Cut in half. Repeat the process six times more to make 14 fringed triple-layer fringes, each 3in (7.5cm) long. You can discard one of them, as you actually need 13.

6 Brush glue along the top edge of the fringed strips. Cut 13 lengths of string, each 3½in (9cm) long. Lay one across a strip, ⅜in (1cm) from the end of the strip, with the end of the string even with the snipped edge. Place a fine knitting needle at the end of the strip. Roll the paper around the needle, then remove the needle and put a blob of glue into the hole it has left. Roll up the other strips in the same way.

Tip: If you can't find double-sided paper, you could glue two pieces of thinner cardstock together. Press them flat under a heavy book while the glue dries, to prevent the paper from warping.

7 Cut 13 strips of purple origami paper, each ⅝ x 1½in (1.5 x 4cm). Apply a little glue to each piece and wind it around the top of a tassel, leaving about ¼in (5mm) protruding over the top where the string enters.

8 Thread the free end of the string on one tassel through one of the holes on the chandelier, bring the string back, and push the free end into the hole in the tassel. Add some more glue and press down the protruding purple paper so that it settles and sticks all around the string. When the glue dries, the string will be secure. Repeat to attach the other tassels to all the holes in the branches and to the bottom hole in the chandelier. Hang the chandelier using the same string threaded through the top hole.

picture frame

This is a quick project—no patterns are used and all the elements are hand cut. To be proficient in papercutting you need to be confident about cutting paper without previously marking a design, and this project provides an excellent way to acquire those skills. I took a picture frame with a wide, flat front, which I had previously covered with pages from an illustrated paperback book about wildflowers, and I covered it with red paper cut into a stylized design. I like the way the subtle illustrations contrast with the bold red decoration.

You will need

Cutting mat and metal ruler
Craft knife or scalpel
Red poster paper (a fine paper with the color on one side only—it comes in large sheets and is the traditional papercutting paper)
Wooden picture frame with a flat front, covered with thin, flexible paper pages cut from an old book (see Tip)
Small, sharp scissors
Spray adhesive

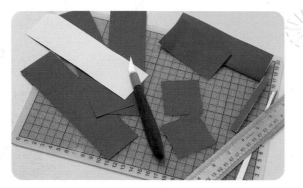

1 Using a cutting mat, metal ruler, and craft knife, cut four squares and four strips from the red paper. The squares should each be about ½in (1.5cm) smaller than the width of the molding—the molding I used is 2½in (6.5cm) wide so I cut 2in (5cm) squares. The width of the four strips should be the same as the squares—so for this frame they were 2in (5cm) wide. The length of two of those strips should be the length of the whole frame less twice the width of the strips less a further 1in (2.5cm). The length of the other two strips should be the width of the whole frame less twice the width of the strips less a further 1in (2.5cm). This frame is 11½in (29cm) square, so the four strips are each 6½in (16.5cm) long.

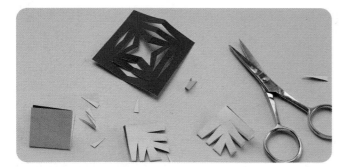

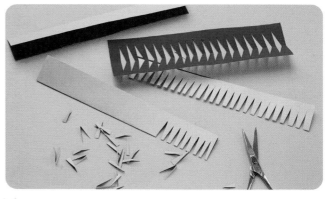

2 Fold one square in half and then in half again. Using small, sharp scissors, cut a V-shape out of the folded corner, cutting slightly less than halfway into the width of the square. Cut two thin triangles out of each of the two adjacent folded edges. The inner triangles—next to the V-shaped cut—should stop slightly before the center of the folded square, and the outer ones should stop the same distance beyond the center. Unfold the square to reveal the design. Repeat for the other three squares.

3 Fold one strip in half lengthwise and cut triangles all along the folded side. The triangles should stop a little beyond halfway across the width. Also, each triangle should have one long right-angled edge and one long slanted edge, with the slanted edge of each triangle parallel to the slanted edges of the others and on the same side. Repeat for the other three strips.

Tip: *To cover the frame with thin, flexible pages cut from an old book prior to decorating it with papercuts, paint slightly diluted white (PVA) glue onto the back of the pages. Stick the pages to the frame, overlapping them and wrapping the edges around the outside. Smooth the paper so it is flat.*

4 Working outdoors or in a well-ventilated space, spray the back of the strips with adhesive. Lay each strip in place centrally on each side of the front of the covered frame, leaving an even margin all around.

5 Stick the square pieces in place at each corner in the same way. Press the red paper down carefully, making sure that the adhesive sticks well.

patterns

To make patterns, either trace or photocopy the templates at full size or enlarge them on a photocopier, as directed.

Lovebird decoration page 56
Full size

Easter rabbit gift tag page 28
Full size

Room garland page 46
Full size

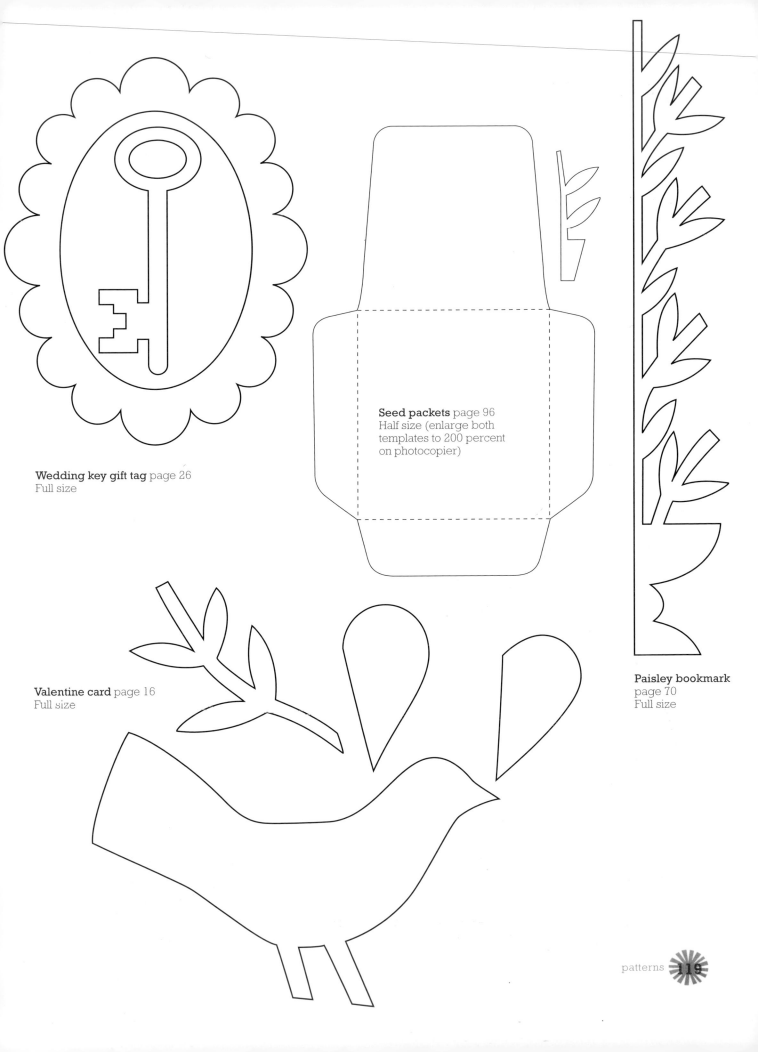

Wedding key gift tag page 26
Full size

Seed packets page 96
Half size (enlarge both
templates to 200 percent
on photocopier)

Valentine card page 16
Full size

Paisley bookmark
page 70
Full size

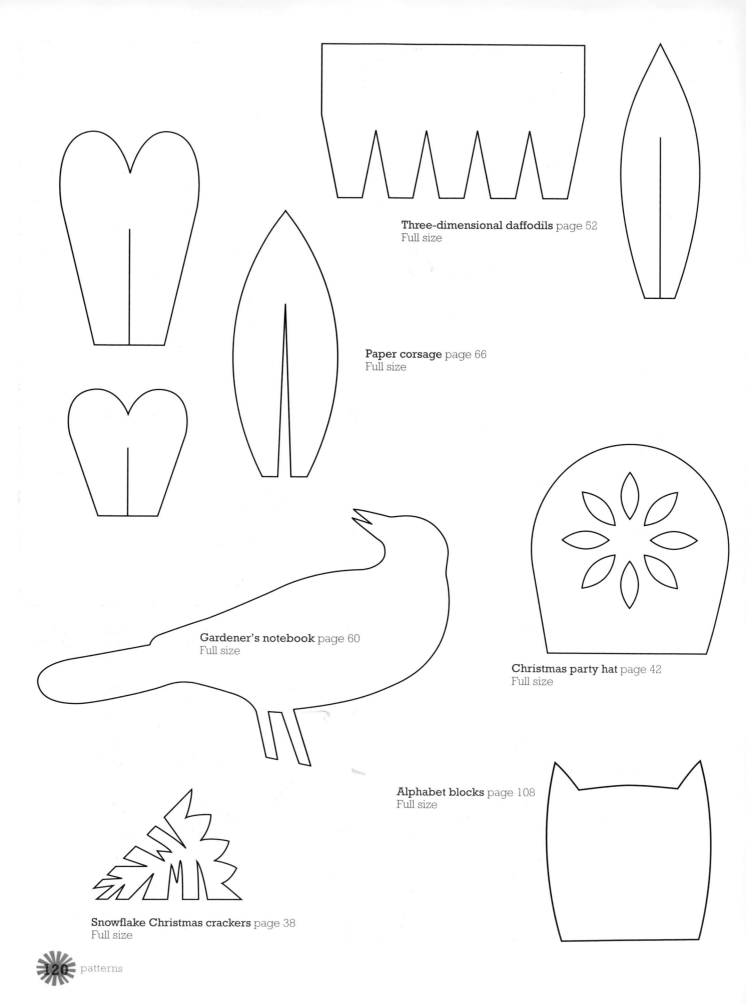

Three-dimensional daffodils page 52
Full size

Paper corsage page 66
Full size

Gardener's notebook page 60
Full size

Christmas party hat page 42
Full size

Alphabet blocks page 108
Full size

Snowflake Christmas crackers page 38
Full size

Decorated eggs page 64
Full size

Greeting card flowers page 12
Full size

Shelf edging page 100
Full size

Change of address card page 20
Half size (enlarge both templates to
200 percent on photocopier)

Blossom frame page 84
Full size

Wise owl growth chart page 80
The tree is one-third size (enlarge to 300 percent on photocopier) and the other four templates are half size (enlarge to 200 percent on photocopier)

Tree of life picture page 88
Half size (enlarge this template to 200 percent on photocopier)

Oval box page 72
Full size

Child's wall frieze page 102
Full size

Contour map starbursts
page 44
Full size

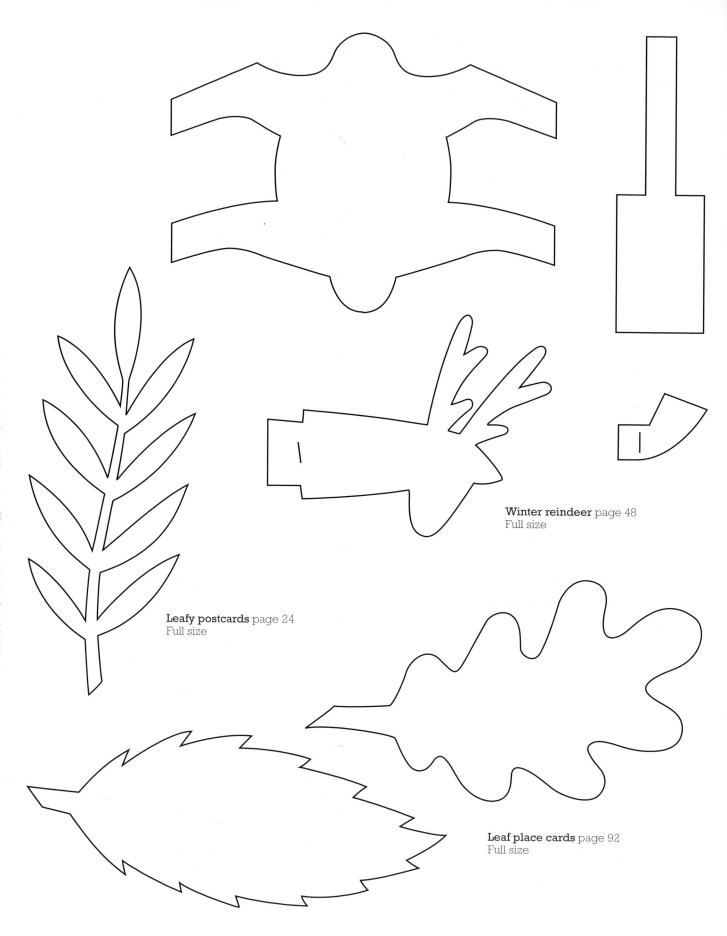

Winter reindeer page 48
Full size

Leafy postcards page 24
Full size

Leaf place cards page 92
Full size

Paper bag lanterns page 36
Full size

Decorated envelope page 31
Half size (enlarge this template to
200 percent on photocopier)

Jam labels page 98
Full size

Table mat page 78
Full size

Paper chandelier page 112
Half size (enlarge to 200 percent
on photocopier)

Papercut peacock page 110
Half size (enlarge all these templates to
200 percent on photocopier)

Butterflies on wire page 106
Full size